JOSSEY-BASS TEACHER

Jossey-Bass Teacher provides educators with practical knowledge and tools to create a positive and lifelong impact on student learning. We offer classroom-tested and research-based teaching resources for a variety of grade levels and subject areas. Whether you are an aspiring, new, or veteran teacher, we want to help you make every teaching day your best.

From ready-to-use classroom activities to the latest teaching framework, our value-packed books provide insightful, practical, and comprehensive materials on the topics that matter most to K–12 teachers. We hope to become your trusted source for the best ideas from the most experienced and respected experts in the field.

The SPELLING Teacher's LESSON-A-DAY

180 Reproducible Activities to Teach Spelling, Phonics, and Vocabulary

Edward B. Fry, Ph.D.

JOSSEY-BASS
A Wiley Imprint
www.josseybass.com

Published by Jossey-Bass
A Wiley Imprint
989 Market Street, San Francisco, CA 94103-1741—www.josseybass.com

Jossey-Bass books and products are available through most bookstores. To contact Jossey-Bass directly call our Customer Care Department within the U.S. at 800-956-7739, outside the U.S. at 317-572-3986, or fax 317-572-4002.

Jossey-Bass also publishes its books in a variety of electronic formats. Some content that appears in print may not be available in electronic books.

ISBN 978-0-470-42980-8

FIRST EDITION

PB Printing   10 9 8 7 6 5 4 3 2

THE AUTHOR

Edward B. Fry, Ph.D., is Professor Emeritus of Education at Rutgers University (New Brunswick, New Jersey), where for twenty-four years he was director of the Reading Center. At Rutgers, Dr. Fry taught graduate and undergraduate courses in reading, curriculum, and other educational subjects and served as chairman and dissertation committee member for doctoral candidates in reading and educational psychology. As the Reading Center's director, he provided instruction for children with reading problems, trained teacher candidates, and conducted statewide reading conferences. Author of the best-selling book *The Reading Teacher's Book of Lists,* Dr. Fry is known internationally for his Readability Graph, which is used by teachers, publishers, and others to judge the reading difficulty of books and other materials. He is also well known for his Instant Words, high-frequency word list, and for reading, spelling, and secondary curriculum materials. He works as a curriculum author and skis and swims whenever possible.

CONTENTS

PART II   CONTRACTIONS, CAPITALIZATION, COMMON MISSPELLINGS, AND MORE

Common Misspellings   **117**

Plurals   **129**

INTRODUCTION

The Spelling Teacher's Lesson-a-Day is aimed at improving the spelling ability of students in Grades 3 to 8, ESL, adult learners, and home-schoolers. The lessons are suitable for classrooms, tutoring, and self-study. Thus, Spelling Review is just that—a review of spelling skills that perhaps should have been learned earlier.

The lessons assume that the student has some spelling ability, but many faulty spelling skills.

A major method is to contrast two or three homophones to show that the same sounds can be spelled differently so the student is learning to spell some useful everyday words, and also the extension of the spelling patterns in those words. The lessons are basically "homophones" and "phonics."

For many students, the second or third homophone will be vocabulary enrichment, and they will learn new words, or new word uses, from the definitions and example sentences.

The reason homophones are important is that many students now write using a computer (word processing and spell check). The problem is that spell check cannot detect an error in meaning (example: peak vs. peek).

However, these lessons also contain many other important spelling skills, such as:

Contractions (they would = they'd)

Capitalization (president vs. President)

Common Misspellings (forth vs. fourth)

Plurals (bench vs. benches)

Abbreviations (Michigan = MI)

Silent Letters (ma_t_ch)

Double Letters (boss)

Suffixes (run vs. running)

Compound Words (roommate vs. room clerk)

Prefixes (a_cc_ident vs. a_dd_ress)

Ending Sounds (act_or_ vs. beg_gar_)

Spelling Problems (ac_tion_ vs. ver_sion_)

Notes for the Teacher

The teacher can select which lesson or section to use. They are not necessarily in a teaching order.

Part of the method in these lessons is to show that many words use similar spelling patterns and, once learned, these patterns will appear in many more complex words. Looking for spelling patterns in words is a useful lifelong habit.

Another plan for these lessons is that they are short and easy so the student won't think of spelling as an onerous chore. "Do you like spelling?" "Yes, it's so easy." Yet these lessons also show the need for precision or correct spelling, as the changing of just a letter or two can change the meaning or pattern.

Getting Started

The teacher can start the lesson by either showing the student a copy of the lesson page or by presenting the lesson orally with the visual aid of the words written on a chalkboard or chart.

1. Discuss and show the homophones and how their spelling differs. Give a few example sentences.

2. Do a bit of review by having the student orally, or in writing, tell the correct homophone spelling for the "Which is right?" sentences in the lesson.

3. Next ask the student to look carefully and perhaps read aloud all the bold print words in the Phonics section.

4. Next, in the Spelling Exercise section, have the student use some or all of the words in the Phonics section and give a little trial test. Call out the words one at a time and use them in a sentence. For clarity you can repeat the word and use it in a sentence. For spelling words, use the homophones and all or selected words from the bold print in the Phonics section.

5. The students can correct their own papers, or the teacher can correct the trial test.

6. Any words misspelled should be written correctly three times.

At a later time the teacher can review several lessons and give a final spelling test.

PART I

HOMOPHONES AND PHONICS LESSONS

1 be vs. bee

be = To take place or happen. *"Will there be any lions at the zoo?"* (v.)

Having a position or place. *"My new desk will be in the corner."* (v.)

bee = An insect with four legs and a stinger. *"That bee is flying in the garden."* (n.)

A social gathering at which people have a task or contest. *"The students have lined up for a spelling bee."* (n.)

Which Is Right?

1. I was just stung by a _____!
2. I'm not sure where the new store will _____ in the mall.
3. Will the new teacher _____ in class today?
4. My grandmother goes to a sewing _____ every Monday.

Phonics: Long E

Learn to spell all the words in bold print.

Pay attention to the same vowel letter pattern in each word.

The Long E sound is sometimes made by the Single E letter pattern.

be	**he**	**me**
we	**she**	**the**

The Long E sound is sometimes made by the Double EE letter pattern.

bee	**fee**	**knee**
lee	**see**	**wee**

Show YOU Know!

1. Write one or two sentences using as many of the words in these Single E and Double EE letter patterns as you can.

2. The teacher or another student will dictate each of these six words for you to write without looking at this page. Use each word in a sentence when it is spoken.

bee	**she**	**me**	**knee**	**be**	**see**

3

2 by vs. bye vs. buy

by = On the side of. *"The wild flowers grew by the side of the road."* (prep.)

The means used. *"The team traveled to the game by bus."* (prep.)

A particular time. *"We plan to arrive at the party by noon."* (prep.)

bye = Short for "goodbye"—often doubled to "bye-bye." *" Bye-bye, I am going home now."* (v.)

buy = To purchase. *"I'm going to the grocery store to buy milk."* (v.)

Which Is Right?

1. The baby waved _____ to me.
2. I drove _____ your house today.
3. He was the first to say _____.
4. I think I'll _____ a new hat at the mall.

Phonics: Long I

Learn to spell all the words in bold print.

Pay attention to the same vowel letter pattern in each word.

The Long I sound is made by the Final Y letter pattern.

by	**my**	**fry**
cry	**dry**	**fly**

The Long I sound is made by the Final YE letter pattern.

bye	**dye**	**eye**
lye	**rye**	**aye**

Show YOU Know!

1. Write one or two sentences using as many of the words in these Final Y and Final YE letter patterns as you can.

2. The teacher or another student will dictate each of these six words for you to write without looking at this page. Use each word in a sentence when it is spoken.

by	**fly**	**eye**	**dye**	**bye**	**cry**

3 fair vs. fare

fair = Going by the rules. *"The judge was very fair."* (adv.)

A show or marketplace taking place outside. *"Our state fair is always crowded."* (n.)

To have a light color. *"That girl has very fair skin."* (adj.)

fare = Money paid for transportation. *"The train fare cost a lot."* (n.)

To progress. *"She did not fare well in the soccer game."* (v.)

Which Is Right?

1. I want to buy a hotdog at the _____.
2. The bus _____ was only $2.00.
3. I don't think the coach's ruling was _____!
4. You should stay out of the sun if you have _____ skin.

Phonics: Long AR

Learn how to spell all the words in bold print.

Pay attention to the same vowel letter pattern in each word.

The Long A plus R sound is made by the AIR letter pattern.

fair	**hair**	**pair**
air	**stair**	**flair**

The Long A plus R sound is made by the ARE letter pattern.

fare	**bare**	**rare**
mare	**square**	**spare**

Show YOU Know!

1. Write one or two sentences using as many of the words in these AIR and ARE letter patterns as you can.

2. The teacher or another student will dictate each of these six words for you to write without looking at this page. Use each word in a sentence when it is spoken.

fare	**pair**	**square**	**air**	**rare**	**fair**

4 no vs. know

no = To deny, refuse, or give a negative response. *"No, I won't go with you to the movie."* (adv.)

know = To have information about. *"I know a lot about dogs and cats."* (v.)

To remember or recall a fact. *"I know where you live."* (v.)

To have an ability. *"I know how to read."* (v.)

Which Is Right?

1. I don't _____ which way to go.
2. There are only two answers to my question, yes or _____.
3. Do you _____ how to ride a bike?
4. _____, I won't tell you the answers to the test!

Phonics: Long O

Learn to spell all the words in bold print. Pay attention to the same vowel letter pattern in each word.

The Long O sound is made by only 3 words with the Single Final O letter pattern.

no	**go**	**so**

The Long O sound is made more often by the Final OW letter pattern.

know	**bow**	**low**	**row**	**mow**	**slow**

The Beginning Sound spelled KN makes the phoneme /n/ as in:

know	**knee**	**knife**

Show YOU Know!

1. Write one or two sentences using as many of the words in these Final O and OW letter patterns as you can.

2. The teacher or another student will dictate each of these six words for you to write without looking at this page. Use each word in a sentence when it is spoken.

know	**go**	**no**	**slow**	**bow**	**so**

6

5 to vs. too vs. two

to = Going in a direction. *"You'll see the hotel if you look <u>to</u> the right."* (prep.)

Going along. *"I'd like <u>to</u> go with you to class."* (prep.)

too = Having more than enough. *"I ate <u>too</u> much candy."* (adv.)

Wanting to also go. *"We want to go, <u>too</u>!"* (adv.)

two = Adding one more to one. *"If you have one apple and one orange, you have <u>two</u> pieces of fruit."* (adj.)

The numeral 2. *"The answer to the first question on the quiz is <u>2</u>+<u>2</u>=4."*

Which is Right?

1. Would you like to play, _____?
2. If you have twins, it means you have _____ of them.
3. Let's all go _____ the park.

Phonics: Long Double OO

Learn to spell all the words in bold print.

Pay attention to the same vowel letter pattern in each word.

The Long Double OO sound is made by the Single Final O letter pattern in only these four common words.

to	**do**	**who**	**two**

The Long Double OO sound is also made by the OO letter pattern.

too	**zoo**	**boo**
goo	**moo**	**woo**

Show YOU Know!

1. Write one or two sentences using as many of the words in these Single O and Double OO letter patterns as you can for this sound.

2. The teacher or another student will dictate each of these six words for you to write without looking at this page. Use each word in a sentence when it is spoken.

too	**who**	**two**	**moo**	**to**	**goo**

6 loan vs. lone

loan = Anything given that must be returned. *"If you'll <u>loan</u> me a pencil, I'll return it at the end of class."* (v.) *"The <u>loan</u> must be paid back."* (n.)

lone = Being alone, solitary. Unaccompanied. *"That old car is the <u>lone</u> vehicle on the road."* (adj.)

Which Is Right?

1. That bird is the _____ survivor of its flock.

2. The man in uniform was the _____ member of the Army at the ceremony.

3. The book was on _____ from the main library.

4. The man asked his friend if he would _____ him some money.

Phonics: Long O

Read aloud all the words in bold print.

Pay attention to the same vowel letter pattern in each word.

The Long O sound is often made by the Final E rule.

lone	**cone**	**stone**
bone	**zone**	**phone**

The Long O sound is also made by the letters OA.

loan   **moan**   **Joan**   **groan**

Show YOU Know!

1. Write one or two sentences using as many of the words in these O plus Final E and OA letter patterns as you can.

2. The teacher or another student will dictate each of these six words for you to write without looking at this page. Use each word in a sentence when it is spoken.

lone   groan   bone   cone   loan   moan

8

tail = The appendage at the back of an animal. *"That dog is wagging his tail."* (n.)

Someone following someone else to track their movements. *"The police officer will tail the criminal."* (n.)

tale = A retelling of something that has happened. *"My father loves to tell a tale from his school years."* (n.)

A lie. *"That boy's excuse for being tardy is just a tale."* (n.)

Which Is Right?

1. *Cinderella* is my favorite fairy _____.
2. That detective will _____ the man all night.
3. That cat's _____ is very furry.
4. The girl told a _____ to try to avoid getting into trouble.

Phonics: Long A

Learn how to spell all the words in bold print.
Pay attention to the same vowel letter pattern in each word.
The Long A sound is made by the AI letter pattern.

tail	**mail**	**jail**
sail	**hail**	**fail**

The Long A sound is also made by the Final E letter pattern.

tale	**sale**
pale	**male**

Show YOU Know!

1. Write one or two sentences using as many of the words in these AI and Final E letter patterns as you can.

2. The teacher or another student will dictate each of these six words for you to write without looking at this page. Use each word in a sentence when it is spoken.

    tail   **jail**   **tale**   **sail**   **sale**   **pale**

8 sea vs. see

sea = A large body of fresh or salt water that is completely or partly enclosed by land. *"This sea has beautiful blue water."*

see = To acknowledge with the eye. *"I see that you have a new dress."* (v.)

To tend to something. *"I will see to it that you are on time."* (v.)

Which Is Right?

1. I would like to _____ the new house.
2. This boat can sail across the _____.
3. The water in the _____ is very cold.
4. Can you _____ the airplane in the sky?

Phonics: Long E

Learn to spell all the words in bold print.

Pay attention to the same vowel letter pattern in each word.

The Long E sound is made by the Double EE in the final position, as we have seen earlier.

see	**free**	**three**
tree	**bee**	**fee**

The Long E sound is also made by the EA letter pattern.

sea	**tea**	**flea**

Show YOU Know!

1. Write one or two sentences using as many of the words in these Double EE and EA letter patterns as you can.

2. The teacher or another student will dictate each of these six words for you to write without looking at this page. Use each word in a sentence when it is spoken.

see	**flea**	**free**	**tea**	**tree**	**sea**

lie = Something told by someone who knows it is untrue. *"I know that what you just said is a lie."* (n.)

To remain flat against a surface. *"That board can lie against the wall until we need it."* (v.)

lye = Mixture of sodium hydroxide and potassium hydroxide that makes a strong alkaline solution. *"My grandmother used lye soap to wash her clothes."* (adj.)

Which s Right?

1. Our teacher made a _____ solution in class.

2. Those test papers can _____ on the desk.

3. That girl just told me a _____.

4. You'll get into trouble if you _____ to your parents.

Phonics: Long I

Learn to spell all the words in bold print.

Pay attention to the same vowel letter pattern in each word.

The Long I sound is made by the IE letter pattern.

lie	**pie**	**tie**	**die**

The Long I sound is also made by the YE letter pattern.

lye	**eye**	**dye**	**rye**

Show YOU Know!

1. Write one or two sentences using as many of the words in these IE and YE letter patterns as you can.

2. The teacher or another student will dictate each of these six words for you to write without looking at this page. Use each word in a sentence when it is spoken.

lye	**pie**	**tie**	**lie**	**eye**	**dye**

10 meat vs. meet

meat = Mammal flesh that is used for food. *"I enjoy eating meat and pota-toes for dinner."* (n.)

meet = To get together face-to-face. *"Let's meet at my house."* (v.)

To make contact with. *"Those two streets meet at the corner."* (v.)

Which Is Right?

1. That group will _____ in my office.

2. Those two halls _____ at the front door.

3. Ground beef is a good _____ for your burger.

4. Vegetarians do not eat _____.

Phonics: Long E

Learn to spell all the words in bold print.

Pay attention to the same vowel letter pattern in each word.

The Long E sound is made by the EA letter pattern.

meat	**beat**	**treat**
eat	**heat**	**seat**

The Long E sound is also made by the Double EE letter pattern.

meet	**greet**	**beet**
feet	**fleet**	**street**

Show YOU Know!

1. Write one or two sentences using as many of the words in these EA and Double EE letter patterns as you can.

2. The teacher or another student will dictate each of these six words for you to write without looking at this page. Use each word in a sentence when it is spoken.

meet	**heat**	**beet**	**street**	**meat**	**eat**

12

11 maid vs. made

maid = A paid female servant. *"The <u>maid</u> cleaned the house very well."* (n.)

made = Something that is formed, created, or built. *"The whole class <u>made</u> presents for the teacher."* (v.)

Which Right?

1. That woman works as a _____ in the hotel.
2. The Girl Scouts _____ a lot of money selling cookies.
3. My friends _____ sweaters for a homeless shelter.
4. The college student would like to work as a _____ during her summer home from school.

Phonics: Long A

Learn to spell all the words in bold print.

Pay attention to the same vowel letter pattern in each word.

The Long A sound is often made by the AI letter pattern.

maid	**paid**	**aid**
staid	**raid**	**braid**

The Long A sound is also made by the Final E letter pattern.

made	**wade**	**grade**
fade	**blade**	**shade**

Show YOU Know!

1. Write one or two sentences using as many of the words in these AI and ADE letter patterns as you can.

2. The teacher or another student will dictate each of these six words for you to write without looking at this page. Use each word in a sentence when it is spoken.

made　**raid**　**blade**　**maid**　**braid**　**grade**

13

12 son vs. sun

son = A male child. *"The woman has both a <u>son</u> and a daughter."* (n.)

sun = A bright star that sustains life on Earth. *"It takes a year for the Earth to rotate around the <u>sun</u>."* (n.)

Which Is Right?

1. I love a bright day when the _____ is shining!
2. My aunt had a _____ last night.
3. What year will her _____ graduate from college?
4. The _____ is part of our solar system.

Phonics: Short U

Learn to spell all the words in bold print.

Pay attention to the same vowel letter pattern in each word.

The Short U sound is made by the letter O only in these words.

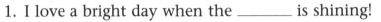

| **son** | **ton** | **won** |

The Short U sound is made by the UN letter pattern.

| **sun** | **fun** | **gun** |
| **run** | **shun** | **spun** |

Show YOU Know!

1. Write one or two sentences using as many of the words in these ON or UN letter patterns as you can.

2. The teacher or another student will dictate each of these six words for you to write without looking at this page. Use each word in a sentence when it is spoken.

| **sun** | **fun** | **ton** | **son** | **run** | **won** |

14

13 dear vs. deer

dear = Anyone or anything that is much loved. *"Her cats were very dear to her."* (adj.)

Word used to express surprise or worry. *"Oh dear, I was so worried about you!"* (interj.)

deer = A swift animal that is related to the elk or moose. *"I saw a deer in the woods."* (n.)

Which Is Right?

1. Did you see the _____ standing by the lake?
2. Oh _____, I was worried that you wouldn't call!
3. On my last hike, I saw both a fox and a _____.
4. My grandmother is very _____ to me.

Phonics: Long E

Learn to spell all the words in bold print.
Pay attention to the same vowel letter pattern in each word.
The Long E sound is made by the Double EE in these words:

deer	**beer**	**jeer**
leer	**peer**	**sneer**

The Long E sound is made by the letters EA in these words:

dear	**fear**	**hear**
near	**rear**	**year**

Show YOU Know!

1. Write one or two sentences using as many of the words in the Long EE and EA letter patterns as you can.
2. The teacher or another student will dictate each of these six words for you to write without looking at this page. Use each word in a sentence when it is spoken.

deer	**year**	**dear**	**peer**	**sneer**	**fear**

do = To perform or carry out as an action. *"We watched her do a dance."* (v.)

To work out, solve. *"He needs time to do his homework."* (v.)

due = Anything that needs to be paid. *"The rent is due next week."* (adj.)

An expected arrival. *"Jack is due to come here today."* (adj.)

dew = Small drops of water, condensing on cool surfaces at night. *"There is dew on the grass every morning."* (n.)

Which Is Right?

1. The class worked together to _____ the puzzle.

2. The leaves of the tree are wet with _____.

3. Your lunch money is _____ today.

4. If you try hard, you can _____ it!

Phonics: Long OO

Learn to spell all the words in bold print. Pay attention to the same vowel letter pattern in each word.

The Long OO sound is made by the letter O in these words:

do   **to**   **who**

The Long OO sound is made by the letters UE in these words:

due   **blue**   **cue**   **glue**   **sue**   **true**

The Long OO sound is made by the letters EW in these words:

dew   **few**   **new**

Show YOU Know!

1. Write one or two sentences using as many of the words in these O, UE, and EW letter patterns as you can.

2. The teacher or another student will dictate each of these six words for you to write without looking at this page. Use each word in a sentence when it is spoken.

dew   **glue**   **do**   **new**   **who**   **due**

16

15 wood vs. would

wood = What lies under the bark of a tree. *"This table is made of <u>wood</u> from an oak tree."* (n.)

Trees that have been chopped down, cut up, and stored for use. *"You need to chop some <u>wood</u> for the fire."* (n.)

would = Past tense of "will." *"He said he <u>would</u> do the laundry."* (H.V.)

To express a situation that might have been if something else had happened. *"We <u>would</u> be done by now if we had started on time."* (H.V.)

Which Is Right?

1. The work _____ be finished by now if you had done it the way I showed you.

2. Can you please put more _____ by the fireplace?

3. _____ from the cherry tree is very beautiful.

4. It _____ make me happy if you came to my party.

Phonics: Long OO

Learn to spell all the words in bold print.
Pay attention to the same vowel letter pattern in each word.
The Long OO sound is made by the Double OO letter pattern.

wood	**good**	**stood**

The Long OO sound is also made by the OU letter pattern.

would	**could**	**should**

Show YOU Know!

1. Write one or two sentences using as many of the words in these OOD and OULD letter patterns as you can.

2. The teacher or another student will dictate each of these six words for you to write without looking at this page. Use each word in a sentence when it is spoken.

would	**could**	**stood**	**wood**	**should**	**good**

16 write vs. right

write = The act of making letters, words, or figures on a surface with a tool such as a pen or pencil. *"I have many letters to <u>write</u>."* (v.)

right = To be in agreement with what is fact or truth. *"It is always <u>right</u> to tell the truth."* (adj.)

The opposite of left. *"Please move your chair to the <u>right</u>."* (adj.)

Which Is Right?

1. I usually _____ letters with my _____ hand.
2. It's not always easy to do the _____ thing.
3. You have to _____ the answers on the test paper.
4. That whole group needs to move to the _____.

Phonics: Long I

Learn to spell all the words in bold print. Pay attention to the same vowel letter pattern in each word.

The Long I sound is made by the Final E letter pattern.

    write   **bite**   **white**   **mite**   **kite**   **quite**

The Long I sound is made by the IGHT letter pattern.

    right   **night**   **fight**   **tight**   **light**   **knight**

The Beginning Sound spelled WR makes the phoneme /r/ as in:

    write   **wrote**   **written**

Show YOU Know!

1. Write one or two sentences using as many of the words in these ITE and IGHT letter patterns as you can.
2. The teacher or another student will dictate each of these six words for you to write without looking at this page. Use each word in a sentence when it is spoken.

    right   **white**   **light**   **bite**   **write**   **tight**

18

17 pole vs. poll

pole = A piece of wood or steel that is usually long and slender. *"There is a pole for the flag in front of the school."* (n.)

The most northern and southern points of the Earth. *"Temperatures at the North and South poles are very similar."* (n.)

poll = The place where voting or registration takes place. *"I will take my mother to the poll early in the morning so she can vote."* (n.)

To gather opinions. *"The school staff took a poll of the students to see how they liked the new lunch menu."* (n.)

Which Is Right?

1. Most penguins live near the South _____.

2. I would like your opinion for this _____ I'm taking.

3. I need a new fishing _____.

4. My father worked at the _____ during the last election.

Phonics: Long O

Learn to spell all the words in bold print. Pay attention to the same vowel letter pattern in each word.

The Long O sound is made by the Final E letter pattern.

| **pole** | **stole** | **hole** | **whole** | **role** | **hole** |

The Long O sound is also made in the OLL letter pattern.

| **poll** | **knoll** | **roll** | **scroll** | **toll** | **stroll** |

Show YOU Know!

1. Write one or two sentences using as many of the words in these OLE and OLL letter patterns as you can.

2. The teacher or another student will dictate each of these six words for you to write without looking at this page. Use each word in a sentence when it is spoken.

| **poll** | **roll** | **hole** | **stroll** | **pole** | **whole** |

18 bear vs. bare

bear = A large mammal with thick hair covering its body and a short tail. *"The bear woke up in his cave."* (n.)

To carry the weight of something. *"She just can't bear the work of having a new job."* (v.)

bare = To be naked or empty. *"The room looks bare with no furniture."* (adj.)

To expose. *"That dog will bare its teeth when it's angry."* (v.)

Which Is Right?

1. I can't _____ the thought of having to move again.
2. I feel _____ without a sweater on my shoulders.
3. I'm hoping to see a _____ during our trip to Alaska!
4. I've moved my desk, so now that corner is _____.

Phonics: Long A

Learn to spell all the words in bold print.
Pay attention to the same vowel letter pattern in each word.
The Long A plus R sound is made by the EAR letter pattern.

bear	**wear**	**swear**

The Long A plus R sound is also made by the ARE letter pattern.

bare	**dare**	**hare**
mare	**rare**	**ware**

Show YOU Know!

1. Write one or two sentences using as many of the words in these EAR and ARE letter patterns as you can.

2. The teacher or another student will dictate each of these six words for you to write without looking at this page. Use each word in a sentence when it is spoken.

bear	**rare**	**mare**	**wear**	**swear**	**dare**

20

19 tax vs. tacks

tax = Money that is paid by citizens to support their government. *"Our tax check must be mailed each year by April 15."* (n.)

tacks = Short, flat-headed nails with sharp tips. *"You can hang up that poster using either tacks or tape."* (n.)

Large, loose stitches used to mark something. *"The tailor tacks in his stitches until the final fitting."* (v.)

Which Is Right?

1. She _____ in the seams until she is ready to finish sewing the dress.

2. The bill in the restaurant includes both _____ and a tip for the waiter.

3. I need more _____ to put these photos up on my bulletin board.

4. My _____ bill seems to get larger each year.

Phonics: Short A

Learn to spell all the words in bold print. Pay attention to the same vowel letter pattern in each word.

The Short A sound is made by the single letter A followed by X.

tax   **lax**   **wax**   **sax**

The Short A sound is also made by the single letter A followed by CK.

tacks   **backs**   **packs**   **sacks**

Show YOU Know!

1. Write one or two sentences using as many of the words in the AX and ACK letter patterns as you can.

2. The teacher or another student will dictate each of these six words for you to write without looking at this page. Use each word in a sentence when it is spoken.

tacks   wax   lax   sacks   tax   backs

20 bite vs. byte

bite = To grip or tear something with the teeth. *"I took a bite of my lunch."* (v.)

A wound made by a bite. *"The red bump is a mosquito bite."* (n.)

byte = An information unit in data processing, usually standing for a letter or number. *"This will only take a few bytes of memory on your computer."* (n.)

Which Is Right?

1. I'm afraid that the snake might _____ my hand.
2. My computer has room for many _____ of information.
3. That boy took a huge _____ of his sandwich.
4. _____ is a common word used when working with computers.

Phonics: Short I

Learn to spell all the words in bold print.
Pay attention to the same vowel letter pattern in each word.
The Short I sound is in the ITE letter pattern.

bite	**kite**	**quite**
site	**mite**	**white**

The Short I sound in the YTE letter pattern occurs in only this word, but it is an important word.

byte

Show YOU Know!

1. Write one or two sentences using as many of the words in these ITE and YTE letter patterns as you can.
2. The teacher or another student will dictate each of these six words for you to write without looking at this page. Use each word in a sentence when it is spoken.

bite   kite   white   byte   quite   site

21 brake vs. break

brake = Something used to slow down or stop a vehicle. *"I use the pedal as a brake on my bicycle."* (n.)

The action of using something to slow or stop a vehicle. *"The car braked at the corner."* (v.)

break = To make something come apart. *"Why did you break that window?"* (v.)

A brief rest or interruption from a task. *"I'm tired and I need to take a break!"* (n.)

Which Is Right?

1. The class will be allowed one _____ during the long test.
2. Please _____ the cookie so we can all have a piece.
3. The pedal on a bicycle is often used as a _____.
4. You need to put your foot on the _____ in order to stop the car.

Phonics: Long A

Learn to spell all the words in bold print. Pay attention to the same vowel letter pattern in each word.

The Long A sound is in the AKE letter pattern.

brake   bake   cake   shake   lake   shake

The Long A sound is in the EAK letter pattern in only two words.

break   steak

The Beginning Sound spelled BR makes the phoneme blend /br/ as in:

bright   bring   broken

Show YOU Know!

1. Write one or two sentences using as many of the words in these AKE and EAK letter patterns as you can.

2. The teacher or another student will dictate each of these six words for you to write without looking at this page. Use each word in a sentence when it is spoken.

break   lake   steak   brake   cake   bake

22 mail vs. male

mail = Packages or envelopes sent through the postal service. *"The mail usually arrives at our office before noon."* (n.)

To send packages or envelopes through the postal service. *"I'm going to mail this letter today."* (v.)

male = The sex of a boy, man, or male animal. *"People often give blue clothes to the parents of a male baby."* (adj.)

Which Is Right?

1. My dog is a _____, but my cat is a female.
2. Finish wrapping that box so you can get it in the _____ today.
3. I have to _____ the invitations to my party.
4. I have three brothers, so almost everyone in my family is _____.

Phonics: Long A

Learn to spell all the words in bold print.
Pay attention to the same vowel letter pattern in each word.
The Long A sound is in the AIL letter pattern.

mail	**tail**	**wail**
snail	**trail**	**frail**

The Long A sound is in the ALE letter pattern.

male	**pale**	**sale**
gale	**hale**	**scale**

Show YOU Know!

1. Write one or two sentences using as many of the words in these AIL and ALE letter patterns as you can.
2. The teacher or another student will dictate each of these six words for you to write without looking at this page. Use each word in a sentence when it is spoken.

mail	**sale**	**scale**	**male**	**snail**	**tail**

24

23 flea vs. flee

flea = Bloodsucking parasite, living on animal flesh. *"My dog keeps scratching at the flea on his back."* (n.)

flee = To run away from or to. *"I watched the woman flee from that burning building."* (v.)

Which Is Right?

1. I'm sure there is a _____ somewhere in my dog's bed.
2. My cat has never had a single _____!
3. The captives would _____ if they could.
4. The crew must _____ the sinking ship.

Phonics: Long E

Learn to spell all the words in bold print.

Pay attention to the same vowel letter pattern in each word.

The Long E sound is made by the EA letter pattern.

flea	**tea**	**sea**
pea	**plea**	

The Long E sound is made by the EE letter pattern.

flee	**bee**	**knee**
see	**tee**	**tree**

Show YOU Know!

1. Write one or two sentences using as many of the words in these EA and EE letter patterns as you can.

2. The teacher or another student will dictate each of these six words for you to write without looking at this page. Use each word in a sentence when it is spoken.

flea	**tree**	**pea**	**see**	**flee**	**sea**

24 shoe vs. shoo

shoe = A durable covering for the foot that often has a rigid heel and sole. *"I had to get a new heel for my left shoe."* (n.)

shoo = To scare or drive away animals or birds. *"I had to shoo away the crows from my garden."* (interj.)

Which Is Right?

1. I often have to _____ the neighbor's cat away from my birdfeeder.

2. When I yelled "_____!", the dog ran away from my path.

3. I can't find the mate to this left _____.

4. The heel on my right _____ is all scuffed up.

Phonics: Long OO

Learn to spell all the words in bold print.

Pay attention to the same vowel letter pattern in each word.

The Long OO sound is made in the Double OO letter pattern.

shoo	**zoo**	**goo**
too	**moo**	**boo**

The Long OO sound, made in the OE letter pattern, occurs in only one word.

shoe

Show YOU Know!

1. Write one or two sentences using as many of the words in these OO and OE letter patterns as you can.

2. The teacher or another student will dictate each of these six words for you to write without looking at this page. Use each word in a sentence when it is spoken.

shoe	**zoo**	**moo**	**boo**	**shoo**	**too**

26

25 cheap vs. cheep

cheap = Inexpensive; costing little. *"Meals at that small restaurant are usually very cheap."* (adj.)

Someone who is not willing to spend money. *"My uncle has always been cheap."* (adj.)

cheep = To chirp. *"Baby birds <u>cheep</u> when they are hungry."* (v.)

Which Is Right?

1. Was that a _____ I heard coming from that nest?

2. I can't believe how _____ this dress was!

3. I know he's _____ because he always avoids paying his portion of the bill.

4. The smallest bird in the nest was able to _____ the loudest.

Phonics: Long E

Learn to spell all the words in bold print. Pay attention to the same vowel letter pattern in each word.

The Long E sound is made by the EEP letter pattern.

> **cheep**   **deep**   **Jeep**   **keep**   **weep**   **peep**

The Long E sound is made by the EAP letter pattern.

> **cheap**   **leap**   **heap**

The Beginning Sound spelled CH makes the phoneme /ch/ as in:

> **child**   **church**   **chance**

Show YOU Know!

1. Write one or two sentences using as many of the words in these EEP and EAP letter patterns as you can.

2. The teacher or another student will dictate each of these six words for you to write without looking at this page. Use each word in a sentence when it is spoken.

> **cheap**   **deep**   **cheep**   **leap**   **weep**   **keep**

26 hall vs. haul

hall = A large building or room used for a specific purpose. *"The party took place in the dining hall."* (n.)

A passageway through a building or house. *"We had to walk down a narrow hall to get to our room."* (n.)

haul = To drag or pull something with force, from one place to another. *"We need to haul those branches out of the front yard."* (v.)

Which Is Right?

1. Just walk down the _____ to the open door.
2. I think we'll need a tractor to _____ those bricks.
3. That large _____ is perfect for the wedding party.
4. Will you help me _____ the sofa into the other room?

Phonics: Broad O

Learn to spell all the words in bold print.
Pay attention to the same vowel letter pattern in each word.
The Broad O sound is made by the ALL letter pattern.

hall	**ball**	**wall**
tall	**call**	**fall**

The Broad O sound is made by the AUL letter pattern in only two words.

haul	**maul**

Show YOU Know!

1. Write one or two sentences using as many of the words in these ALL and AUL letter patterns as you can.

2. The teacher or another student will dictate each of these six words for you to write without looking at this page. Use each word in a sentence when it is spoken.

hall	**call**	**wall**	**ball**	**maul**	**haul**

27 leak vs. leek

leak = A crack or hole that lets something in or out. *"Water can <u>leak</u> out of that hole in the bucket."* (v.)

leek = A vegetable resembling an onion. *"Using a <u>leek</u> in the soup will give it a nice flavor."* (n.)

Which Is Right?

1. Please get me two potatoes and one _____ when you go to the grocery store.

2. We need to find the _____ in the water pipe.

3. If you put a _____ in the pot with the other vegetables, you'll have a wonderful stew.

4. If you don't fix that crack in the wall, moisture will _____ in from the outside.

Phonics: Long E

Learn to spell all the words in bold print.

Pay attention to the same vowel letter pattern in each word.

The Long E sound is made with the EAK letter pattern.

leak	**peak**	**weak**
speak	**freak**	**creak**

The Long E sound is made with the EEK letter pattern.

leek	**seek**	**week**
peek	**cheek**	**Greek**

Show YOU Know!

1. Write one or two sentences using as many of the words in these EAK and EEK letter patterns as you can.

2. The teacher or another student will dictate each of these six words for you to write without looking at this page. Use each word in a sentence when it is spoken.

leek   weak   week   peak   speak   peek

28 roll vs. role

roll = To move or push forward on a surface by constantly turning over. *"The boy can roll the ball all around the room."* (v.)

A small piece of baked, rounded yeast dough. *"Can you buy me a roll while you're at the grocery store?"* (n.)

role = A character portrayed by an actor in a performance. *"This is the largest role that I've ever had in a play."* (n.)

Which Is Right?

1. I hope you get the _____ you want in the school musical.
2. That actor plays a mean _____ in a television series.
3. I love to eat a warm _____ with butter with my dinner.
4. Please _____ the exercise ball over to the other side of the gym.

Phonics: Long O

Learn to spell all the words in bold print.
Pay attention to the same vowel letter pattern in each word.
The Long O sound is made by the OLL letter pattern.

roll	**poll**	**toll**
stroll	**knoll**	**scroll**

The Long O sound is made by the OLE letter pattern.

role	**mole**	**sole**
hole	**pole**	**stole**

Show YOU Know!

1. Write one or two sentences using as many of the words in these OLL and OLE letter patterns as you can.
2. The teacher or another student will dictate each of these six words for you to write without looking at this page. Use each word in a sentence when it is spoken.

role	**stroll**	**stole**	**toll**	**roll**	**pole**

30

29 die vs. dye

die = To become dead; stop living. *"Everything that is living has to die, sooner or later."* (v.)

To lose strength or force. *"The force of the rainstorm will die down as it passes through town."* (v.)

dye = Liquid or powder color used to change the color of something else. *"I'm going to use dye to darken the color of this blue dress."* (n.)

To change the color of something. *"That woman pays a lot of money to dye her hair at a salon."* (v.)

Which Is Right?

1. Sometimes food, such as blueberries or cranberries, is used to _____ cloth.

2. After a while, the applause will _____ down.

3. That plant will _____ if you forget to water it.

4. This _____ is a beautiful color of green.

Phonics: Long I

Learn to spell all the words in bold print. Pay attention to the same vowel letter pattern in each word.

The Long I sound is in the IE letter pattern.

die	**lie**	**pie**	**tie**

The Long I sound is in the YE letter pattern.

dye	**bye**	**eye**	**aye**	**rye**	**lye**

Show YOU Know!

1. Write one or two sentences using as many of the words in the IE and YE letter patterns as you can.

2. The teacher or another student will dictate each of these six words for you to write without looking at this page. Use each word in a sentence when it is spoken.

die	**pie**	**eye**	**bye**	**dye**	**tie**

30 led vs. lead

led = Past tense of "lead" (to go before). *"The teacher led the students back into the classroom after the fire drill."* (v.)

lead = A soft metallic element. *"Divers often use lead weights."* (n.)

Which Is Right?

1. Most pencils have a _____ center.

2. My purse is large and feels as heavy as _____!

3. The teacher _____ the class in a game of "Simon Says."

4. One path _____ the children into the woods, while the other path went directly into town.

Phonics: Short E

Learn to spell all the words in bold print.

Pay attention to the same vowel letter pattern in each word.

The Short E sound is made by the ED letter pattern.

led	**fed**	**sped**
red	**bed**	**bled**

The Short E sound is made by the EAD letter pattern.

lead	**head**	**read**	**dead**

Show YOU Know!

1. Write one or two sentences using as many of the words in these ED and EAD letter patterns as you can.

2. The teacher or another student will dictate each of these six words for you to write without looking at this page. Use each word in a sentence when it is spoken.

lead	**bed**	**head**	**red**	**led**	**read**

32

31 eight vs. ate

eight = The number 8. *"Seven plus one is eight."* (n.)

ate = Past tense of "eat." *"I ate a sandwich for lunch."* (v.)

Which Is Right?

1. I think _____ people can sit at this table.
2. You can't be hungry. You just _____ dinner!
3. That young child can count to _____!
4. We _____ at a wonderful restaurant last night.

Phonics: Long A

Learn to spell all the words in bold print.

Pay attention to the same vowel letter pattern in each word.

The Long A sound is made by the EI letter pattern. This is unique; it does not occur in any other common words.

eight

The Long A sound is also made by the ATE (Final E) letter pattern.

ate	**date**	**fate**	**gate**
hate	**late**	**mate**	**rate**

Show YOU Know!

1. Write one or two sentences using as many of the words in these EI and ATE letter patterns as you can.

2. The teacher or another student will dictate each of these six words for you to write without looking at this page. Use each word in a sentence when it is spoken.

eight	**hate**	**late**	**rate**	**ate**	**date**

32 I vs. eye

I = Personal pronoun. The person talking. *"Jane and I are going to the store."* (pron.)

eye = A part of the body used for sight. *"My mom had surgery on her right eye."* (n.)

The calm, quiet center of a hurricane. *"The safest place to be in a hurricane is in the eye."* (n.)

Which Is Right?

1. That camera was able to show us what the _____ of a hurricane looks like.
2. You and _____ are a lot alike.
3. _____ think we should go to a movie tomorrow.
4. I think I have some dust in my _____.

Phonics: Long I

Learn to spell all the words in bold print.

Pay attention to the same vowel letter pattern in each word.

The Long I sound is made by the I letter pattern. This is unique. There is only one word like this; incidentally it is one of the shortest words in the English language. The other shortest word is "a," as in "a book."

I

The Long I sound is also made by the YE letter pattern, as in:

eye	**bye**	**dye**
lye	**rye**	**aye**

Show YOU Know!

1. Write one or two sentences using as many of the words in these I and YE letter patterns as you can.
2. The teacher or another student will dictate each of these six words for you to write without looking at this page. Use each word in a sentence when it is spoken.

eye	**bye**	**I**	**dye**	**lye**	**rye**

34

33 ball vs. bawl

ball = Round object of any size and material, used in games. *"The ball rolled into the street."* (n.)

A pitched ball in a baseball game that does not go over home plate between the batter's knees and shoulders. *"The count in the baseball game was one ball and two strikes."* (n.)

bawl = To cry loudly and uncontrollably. *"I heard the child bawl when she fell on the sidewalk."* (v.)

Which Is Right?

1. You only skinned your knee, so please don't _____.
2. If he throws another _____, the pitcher will be taken out of the game.
3. Will you throw the _____ to me so we can start the soccer game?
4. When you _____ like that, I can't understand what you're saying!

Phonics: Broad O

Learn to spell all the words in bold print. Pay attention to the same vowel letter pattern in each word.

The Broad O sound is made by the ALL letter pattern.

ball   tall   call   wall   fall   mall   hall

The Broad O sound is also made by the AWL letter pattern.

bawl   brawl   crawl   shawl   drawl   sprawl

Show YOU Know!

1. Write one or two sentences using as many of the words in these ALL and AWL letter patterns as you can.
2. The teacher or another student will dictate each of these six words for you to write without looking at this page. Use each word in a sentence when it is spoken.

ball   fall   drawl   tall   bawl   shawl

34 base vs. bass

base = The foundation of something. *"The base of this house is made of cement."* (n.)

One of four corners on a baseball diamond. *"Jimmy ran from second base to third."* (n.)

bass = A deep tone. *"John plays the bass drum in the band."* (adj.)

Which Is Right?

1. The _____ of the flagpole is made of a very heavy metal.
2. If you sing the _____ part in the choir, your voice must be very low.
3. The _____ section of the chorus is usually all men.
4. If he can run to home _____, he'll score a point and the game will be tied!

Phonics: Long A

Learn to spell all the words in bold print.
Pay attention to the same vowel letter pattern in each word.
The Long A sound is made by the ASE letter pattern.

| **base** | **case** | **vase** | **chase** |

The Long A sound is also made by the ASS letter pattern in only one other word:

bass

Show YOU Know!

1. Write one or two sentences using as many of the words in these ASE and ASS letter patterns as you can.
2. The teacher or another student will dictate each of these five words for you to write without looking at this page. Use each word in a sentence when it is spoken.

| **base** | **case** | **bass** | **vase** | **chase** |

35 week vs. weak

week = A period of seven days, one after another. *"I get paid at the end of each week."* (n.)

weak = Without power or strength. *"My cell phone has a very weak signal on this street."* (adj.)

Which Is Right?

1. I broke my leg last year, and it still feels very _____.
2. I plan to take a vacation for a full _____.
3. There is just one _____ before the start of summer vacation!
4. I begin to feel _____ if I don't eat breakfast.

Phonics: Long E

Learn to spell all the words in bold print.

Pay attention to the same vowel letter pattern in each word.

The Long E sound is made by the Double EE letter pattern.

week	**peek**	**seek**	**meek**
Greek	**creek**	**sleek**	**cheek**

The Long E sound is also made by the EA letter pattern.

weak	**leak**	**peak**	**teak**
creak	**sneak**	**freak**	**bleak**

Show YOU Know!

1. Write one or two sentences using as many of these EE and EA letter patterns as you can.
2. The teacher or another student will dictate each of these six words for you to write without looking at this page. Use each word in a sentence when it is spoken.

weak	**cheek**	**sneak**	**creek**	**week**	**freak**

not = Negative; another way of saying no. *"I am not going shopping today."* (adv.)

knot = Tying rope or string together. *"I learned how to tie a square knot when I was a Scout."* (n.)

Which Is Right?

1. You will _____ be able to run with that sprained ankle.
2. Will you tie a _____ in this cord for me?
3. I will _____ be able to answer the phone this morning.
4. It's hard to untie my shoe when the _____ is too tight.

Phonics: Short O

Learn to spell all the words in bold print.
Pay attention to the same vowel letter pattern in each word.
The Short O sound is made by the OT letter pattern.

not	**got**	**hot**	**lot**
shot	**spot**	**pot**	**rot**

Note that the Beginning Sound in the word "knot" is spelled KN and makes the phoneme /n/ as in:

knot	**knew**	**know**	**knife**
knight	**knock**	**knit**	**knuckle**

Show YOU Know!

1. Write one or two sentences using as many of the words in the OT and KN letter patterns as you can.
2. The teacher or another student will dictate each of these six words for you to write without looking at this page. Use each word in a sentence when it is spoken.

knot   knew   shot   knife   not   spot

37 rain vs. reign

rain = Water drops that fall from the sky. *"The weather forecast calls for rain tomorrow."* (n.)

reign = A period of royal rule. *"The Queen of England has had a reign of many years."* (n.)

Which Is Right?

1. I like to take an umbrella and walk in the _____.
2. I'm reading about a King of England whose _____ included several wars.
3. If the _____ doesn't stop, we won't be able to go on a hike.
4. Queen Elizabeth has had a long _____.

Phonics: Long A

Learn to spell all the words in bold print.
Pay attention to the same vowel letter pattern in each word.
The Long A sound is made by the AI letter pattern.

rain	**main**	**pain**	**vain**
brain	**chain**	**drain**	**grain**

The Long A sound made by the EIGN letter pattern occurs in only one common word:

reign

Show YOU Know!

1. Write one or two sentences using as many of the words in the AIN and EIGN letter patterns as you can.
2. The teacher or another student will dictate each of these six words for you to write without looking at this page. Use each word in a sentence when it is spoken.

rain   **grain**   **reign**   **brain**   **main**   **pain**

38 plain vs. plane

plain = Anything simple, without much design. *"I like this dress, even though it's quite plain."* (adj.)

Something that is easily seen, understood, or heard. *"It's plain to see that he loves to play the piano."* (adj.)

plane = Shortened form of the word "airplane." *"That is the largest plane that I've ever seen!"* (adj.)

A tool with a blade that's used to shape or smooth wood. *"The carpenter used a plane to make the wood smooth."* (adj.)

Which Is Right?

1. If I had a _____, I could smooth down this tabletop.
2. If we take a _____, we could be home much faster.
3. He speaks in a very _____ manner; it's easy to understand what he's saying.
4. With a colorful sofa, this room won't seem _____.

Phonics: Long A

Learn to spell all the words in bold print. Pay attention to the same vowel letter pattern in each word.

The Long A sound is made by the AIN letter pattern.

plain	**Spain**	**stain**	**strain**
train	**slain**	**drain**	**main**

The Long A sound is also made by the ANE letter pattern.

plane	**cane**	**Jane**	**lane**
mane	**pane**	**sane**	**vane**

Show YOU Know!

1. Write one or two sentences using as many of the words in the AIN and ANE letter patterns as you can.
2. The teacher or another student will dictate each of these six words for you to write without looking at this page. Use each word in a sentence when it is spoken.

plane	**main**	**strain**	**lane**	**plain**	**train**

39 past vs. passed

past = A point in time that has already happened. *"This photo album is filled with memories of the past."* (n.)

passed = Past tense of the word "pass." *"Summer vacation has passed, and school begins again tomorrow!"* (v.)

Which Is Right?

1. He _____ all of his exams, so next year he will be entering high school.
2. This _____ July I celebrated my 16th birthday.
3. I _____ my best friend in the school hallway every day last year.
4. I have many happy memories of the _____.

Phonics: Short A

Learn to spell all the words in bold print.

Pay attention to the same vowel letter pattern in each word.

The Short A sound is made by the AST letter pattern.

past	**cast**	**fast**	**last**
mast	**vast**	**blast**	

The Short A sound is also made by the ASSED letter pattern. This occurs in only one word:

passed

Show YOU Know!

1. Write one or two sentences using as many of the words in the AST and ASSED letter patterns as you can.
2. The teacher or another student will dictate each of these six words for you to write without looking at this page. Use each word in a sentence when it is spoken.

passed **fast** **last** **blast** **past** **cast**

40 or vs. oar

or = Express a choice. *"You must study or you will not do well on the test."* (conj.)

Explains that two things are similar. *"You can have either cake or cookies after your meal."* (conj.)

oar = A long pole with a wide end used to row a boat. *"If each of us takes an oar, rowing the boat will be much easier."* (n.)

1. We can rent either a van _____ a small truck to help with the move.
2. You apologize to your sister _____ you must go to your room!
3. The wooden _____ is very heavy.
4. This old rowboat is missing one _____.

Phonics: Broad O

Learn to spell all the words in bold print.

Pay attention to the same vowel letter pattern in each word.

The Broad O sound is made by the OR letter pattern. This occurs in only one word:

or

The Broad O sound is also made by the OAR letter pattern.

oar   **roar**   **soar**   **boar**

Show YOU Know!

1. Write one or two sentences using as many of the words in the OR and OAR letter patterns as you can.
2. The teacher or another student will dictate each of these five words for you to write without looking at this page. Use each word in a sentence when it is spoken.

oar   **boar**   **roar**   **or**   **soar**

41 beach vs. beech

beach = Sand or pebbles along a seashore. *"I like to collect seashells on the* <u>*beach*</u>.*"* (n.)

To run a boat or sea-animal onto the sand. *"The Coast Guard tried to* <u>*beach*</u> *the injured whale in order to save its life."* (v.)

beech = A tree with smooth, gray bark. *"This beautiful wood comes from a* <u>*beech*</u> *tree."* (adj.)

The sweet nut that grows on a beech tree. *"These* <u>*beech*</u> *nuts are very good to eat."* (n.)

Which Is Right?

1. The table in my living room is made of _____ wood.
2. I like to go to the _____ when I'm on vacation.
3. They're trying to _____ the damaged boat before it sinks.
4. My mother made some wonderful muffins that had _____ nuts in them.

Phonics: Long E

Learn to spell all the words in bold print.
Pay attention to the same vowel letter pattern in each word.
The Long E sound is made in the EACH letter pattern.

beach	**reach**	**peach**	**leach**
teach	**bleach**	**preach**	**breach**

The Long E sound is also made by the EECH letter pattern.

beech	**leech**	**screech**

Show YOU Know!

1. Write one or two sentences using as many of the words in the EACH and EECH letter patterns as you can.
2. The teacher or another student will dictate each of these six words for you to write without looking at this page. Use each word in a sentence when it is spoken.

beach	**reach**	**teach**	**beech**	**preach**	**bleach**

row = Objects lined up next to each other in a straight line. *"You can find your seat in the second row."* (n.)

To propel or steer with oars. *"We can row to the other side of the lake in less than an hour."* (v.)

roe = The eggs of a fish. *"Many roe were found in the fish we caught."* (n.)

Which Is Right?

1. Salmon _____ is a very bright red color.
2. Will you _____ the boat for a while?
3. The class was asked to stand in a straight _____.
4. If you compare the _____ of several fish, you'll see that they're different in size and color.

Phonics: Long O

Learn to spell all the words in bold print.

Pay attention to the same vowel letter pattern in each word.

The Long O sound is made by the OW letter pattern.

row	**low**	**mow**	**slow**
sow	**glow**	**grow**	**show**

The Long O sound is also made by the OE letter pattern.

roe	**doe**	**hoe**	**toe**
woe	**Joe**	**foe**	

Show YOU Know!

1. Write one or two sentences using as many of the words in the OW and OE letter patterns as you can.

2. The teacher or another student will dictate each of these six words for you to write without looking at this page. Use each word in a sentence when it is spoken.

row	**show**	**woe**	**foe**	**toe**	**low**

43 pause vs. paws

pause = A brief halt. *"There was a pause in the ceremony while the speaker found his speech."* (v.)

paws = Animal feet. *"That bear caught a fish with its paws."* (n.)

1. That puppy has very large _____!
2. If we can _____ our conversation for a minute, I'd like to get a glass of water.
3. I can see the prints of the cat's _____ in the dirt.
4. There was a _____ in the music while the DJ made an announcement.

Phonics: Broad O

Learn to spell all the words in bold print.

Pay attention to the same vowel letter pattern in each word.

The Broad O sound is made in the AWS letter pattern.

paws	**laws**	**saws**
jaws	**gnaws**	

Note that the Beginning Sound in the word "gnaws" is spelled GN and makes the phoneme /n/ as in:

gnaw   **gnat**   **gnarl**   **gnome**

Show YOU Know!

1. Write one or two sentences using as many of the words in the AWS letter pattern as you can.
2. The teacher or another student will dictate each of these six words for you to write without looking at this page. Use each word in a sentence when it is spoken.

paws   **laws**   **pause**   **saws**   **gnaws**   **jaws**

44 oh vs. owe

oh = An expression of emotion resulting from anger, pain, fear, or surprise. *"Oh, I'm surprised to see you up this early."* (interj.)

owe = To be indebted to someone or something. *"I owe you so much for all you've done for me."* (v.)

Which Is Right?

1. I'd like to give you the dollar that I _____ you.

2. _____, I can't believe you just said that to me!

3. My sister said "_____!" in a loud voice when the lights went out.

4. I _____ a big "thank you" to my father for teaching me how to swim.

Phonics: Long O

Learn to spell all the words in bold print.

Pay attention to the same vowel letter pattern in each word.

The Long O sound is made by the OH letter pattern in only one word:

oh

The Long O sound is also made by the OWE letter pattern in only one word:

owe

Show YOU Know!

1. Write one or two sentences using as many of the words in the OH and OWE letter patterns as you can.

2. The teacher or another student will dictate each of these two words for you to write without looking at this page. Use each word in a sentence when it is spoken.

oh   owe

45 beat vs. beet

beat = To strike or stir over and over. *"Add eggs and <u>beat</u> for two minutes."* (v.)

To defeat. *"We have to <u>beat</u> this team if we want to go to the playoffs."* (v.)

beet = A plant with red roots used as a vegetable, and with white roots used for sugar. *"I had a cooked red <u>beet</u> with my dinner."* (n.)

Which Is Right?

1. My mother makes a wonderful _____ soup.
2. He'll keep a _____ to the music with his drum.
3. I think my high school basketball team will _____ the visiting team.
4. My grocery list includes two potatoes, a turnip, and a _____.

Phonics: Long E

Learn to spell all the words in bold print.
Pay attention to the same vowel letter pattern in each word.
The Long E sound is made in the EAT letter pattern.

beat	**eat**	**heat**	**meat**
neat	**seat**	**peat**	**feat**

The Long E sound is also made in the EET letter pattern.

beet	**feet**	**meet**	**fleet**
greet	**sheet**	**street**	**sweet**

Show YOU Know!

1. Write one or two sentences using as many of the words in the EAT and EET letter patterns as you can.
2. The teacher or another student will dictate each of these six words for you to write without looking at this page. Use each word in a sentence when it is spoken.

beet	**sweet**	**neat**	**sheet**	**beat**	**meat**

46 pier vs. peer

pier = A structure that extends out into the water and is used as a place for ships to dock. *"Many boats are docked at that big pier."* (n.)

peer = A person of the same age, class, or rank. *"That girl and I are the same age, so she is a peer of mine."* (n.)

Which Is Right?

1. I am a _____ of these two classmates.
2. This weekend we went down to the local _____ to rent a boat.
3. It would be interesting to know how that _____ was built out over the water.
4. That soldier is a _____ of the other men in his army squad.

Phonics: Long E

Learn to spell all the words in bold print.

Pay attention to the same vowel letter pattern in each word.

The Long E sound is made in the IER letter pattern.

pier   **tier**

The Long E sound is also made in the EER letter pattern.

peer	**deer**	**jeer**	**leer**
beer	**sheer**	**sneer**	**steer**

Show YOU Know!

1. Write one or two sentences using as many of the words in the IER and EER letter patterns as you can.
2. The teacher or another student will dictate each of these six words for you to write without looking at this page. Use each word in a sentence when it is spoken.

pier   **deer**   **sheer**   **peer**   **tier**   **sneer**

47 hole vs. whole

hole = An opening or space within something. *"The men were digging a hole in the backyard for a new swimming pool."* (n.)

whole = Full or complete. *"I was full after eating the whole meal."* (adj.)

1. The _____ class is going on a field trip to the museum.
2. I need someone to dig a _____ so we can plant this lemon tree.
3. The _____ quiz was hard, but I thought question number 8 was particularly difficult.
4. I just noticed that my favorite shirt has a _____ in the sleeve!

Phonics: Long O

Learn to spell all the words in bold print.

Pay attention to the same vowel letter pattern in each word.

The Long O sound is made in the OLE letter pattern.

hole	**dole**	**pole**	**role**
sole	**stole**	**mole**	**whole**

Note that the Beginning Sound in the word "whole" is spelled WH and makes the phoneme /h/ as in:

whole

The same sound is also spelled H in "hole."

Show YOU Know!

1. Write one or two sentences using as many of the words in the H and WH beginning letter patterns as you can.
2. The teacher or another student will dictate each of these six words for you to write without looking at this page. Use each word in a sentence when it is spoken.

whole	**role**	**hole**	**pole**	**mole**	**stole**

48 which vs. witch

which = Word used to ask questions about people or things. *"Which plane are you taking to New York?"* (pron.)

witch = A woman believed to have magical, supernatural power. *"In this story the witch helps the children find their way home."* (n.)

Which Is Right?

1. The _____ in this story is very wicked.
2. On _____ side of the room do you want your desk?
3. _____ cereal do you like to eat in the morning?
4. In the play we saw, the _____ wore a black, pointy hat.

Phonics: Short I

Learn to spell all the words in bold print. Pay attention to the same vowel letter pattern in each word.

The Short I sound is made in the ITCH letter pattern.

witch	**ditch**	**pitch**	**twitch**
switch	**snitch**	**hitch**	**stitch**

The Short I sound is also made by the ICH letter pattern.

which   **rich**

Note that the Beginning Sound in the word "witch" is spelled W and makes the phoneme /w/ as in:

witch   **will**   **win**   **wire**

And the Beginning Sound of "which" makes almost the same sound /h/ or /hw/—in fact, many people do not say or hear any difference.

Show YOU Know!

1. Write one or two sentences using as many of the words in the ITCH and ICH letter patterns as you can.
2. The teacher or another student will dictate each of these six words for you to write without looking at this page. Use each word in a sentence when it is spoken.

which   **twitch**   **rich**   **witch**   **ditch**   **pitch**

49 hail vs. hale

hail = A combination of ice and snow formed into a small ball that falls like rain. *"The hail dented my car."* (n.)

A gesture or motion used to attract attention. *"It is difficult to hail a taxi in the rain."* (v.)

hale = To be free from sickness. *"He is hale and hardy and never catches the flu."* (adj.)

Which Is Right?

1. If we can _____ a taxi, we can still get to the theater on time.
2. I don't want to leave the house during this _____ storm.
3. When I eat a balanced diet, I feel _____ and full of energy!
4. My class is _____ and has an excellent attendance record.

Phonics: Long A

Learn to spell all the words in bold print.
Pay attention to the same vowel letter pattern in each word.
The Long A sound is made in the AIL letter pattern.

hail	**fail**	**bail**	**quail**
sail	**mail**	**rail**	**pail**

The Long A sound is also made by the ALE letter pattern.

hale	**sale**	**shale**	**scale**
tale	**male**	**gale**	**bale**

Show YOU Know!

1. Write one or two sentences using as many of the words in the AIL and ALE letter patterns as you can.

2. The teacher or another student will dictate each of these six words for you to write without looking at this page. Use each word in a sentence when it is spoken.

hail	**scale**	**sail**	**mail**	**hale**	**tale**

50 guest vs. guessed

guest = Someone entertained or received whose needs are provided for. *"As a guest at this hotel, everything will be provided for you."* (n.)

A person invited to participate in an event or activity. *"The governor of our state is the guest of honor at this dinner."* (n.)

guessed = A judgment or opinion formed with little knowledge. *"He guessed at the answer because he didn't study."* (v.)

Which Is Right?

1. At the fair there was a man who _____ people's weight.
2. I just _____ at your shoe size when I bought you these running shoes.
3. I'd like to give you this ticket so that you can come with me as my _____.
4. I want to clean up the extra bedroom because I have a _____ arriving to stay the weekend.

Phonics: Short E

Learn to spell all the words in bold print.
Pay attention to the same vowel letter pattern in each word.
The Short E sound is made in the UEST letter pattern.

guest   **quest**

The Short E sound is also made by the UESSED letter pattern in only this word:

guessed

Show YOU Know!

1. Write one or two sentences using as many of the words in the UEST and UESSED letter patterns as you can.
2. The teacher or another student will dictate each of these three words for you to write without looking at this page. Use each word in a sentence when it is spoken.

guest   **guessed**   **quest**

51 sell vs. cell

sell = To exchange an object for money. *"Susan wanted to <u>sell</u> her house."* (v.)

cell = A small room in a prison. *"The prisoner was forced to stay in this <u>cell</u> for six months."* (n.)

The basic microscopic unit of any living thing. *"Your body is made up of billions of tiny <u>cells</u>."* (n.)

Which Is Right?

1. The scientist spent his day studying one single _____.
2. They only _____ used books at our local bookshop.
3. The inmate's _____ was small but clean.
4. I'm trying to _____ my stamp collection on eBay.

Phonics: Short E

Learn how to spell all the words in bold print. Pay attention to the same vowel letter pattern in each word.

The Short E sound is made in the ELL letter pattern.

sell	**cell**	**bell**	**fell**
knell	**tell**	**well**	**yell**

Note that the Beginning Sound in the word "cell" is spelled C and makes the phoneme /s/. The letter C usually makes the /s/ sound before I, E, and Y, as in:

cell	**cent**	**century**	**city**

The letter C usually makes the /k/ sound before A, O, and U, as in:

cat	**come**	**cool**	**cut**

Show YOU Know!

1. Write one or two sentences using as many of the words in the ELL letter pattern as you can.

2. The teacher or another student will dictate each of these six words for you to write without looking at this page. Use each word in a sentence when it is spoken.

cell	**well**	**city**	**yell**	**sell**	**cat**

52 cents vs. sense

cents = Pennies. *"I bought a book for twenty-five cents."* (n.)

sense = Any of the five senses (smell, touch, sight, hearing, taste). *"My sense of smell is very good."* (n.)

Able to understand and think clearly. *"Your idea shows that you have good sense."* (n.)

Which Is Right?

1. My _____ of sight is so good that I can read every word on the board.
2. That candy costs just a few _____.
3. Your _____ of hearing is bad if you can't hear that siren.
4. If you save a lot of _____, you can end up with dollars!

Phonics: Short E

Learn to spell all the words in bold print. Pay attention to the same vowel letter pattern in each word.

The Short E sound is made in the ENT letter pattern.

cents　　**dents**　　**rents**　　**tents**

The Short E sound is also made in the ENSE letter pattern.

sense　　　**dense**　　　**tense**

Note that the Beginning Sound in the "cent" is spelled C and makes the phoneme /s/, as in:

center　　　**certain**　　　**celery**

See Lesson 51: Note on letter C before I, E, and Y.

Show YOU Know!

1. Write one or two sentences using as many of the words in the ENT and ENSE letter patterns as you can.
2. The teacher or another student will dictate each of these six words for you to write without looking at this page. Use each word in a sentence when it is spoken.

cents　　**tense**　　**tents**　　**dense**　　**sense**　　**rents**

53 bread vs. bred

bread = Food made of a baked dough. *"You can buy <u>bread</u> at the grocery store."* (n.)

bred = To reproduce for a purpose. *"This dog was <u>bred</u> for shows."* (v.)

Which Is Right?

1. Some animals are _____ in zoos.
2. This poodle was _____ to be a show dog.
3. This _____ is hard and stale.
4. That bakery has wonderful _____ for sale.

Phonics: Short E

Learn to spell all the words in bold print.

Pay attention to the same vowel letter pattern in each word.

The Short E sound is made in the EAD letter pattern.

bread	**read**	**lead**	**head**
spread	**thread**	**tread**	**dead**

The Short E sound is also made in the ED letter pattern.

bred	**red**	**bled**	**shred**
sped	**sled**	**fed**	**wed**

Show YOU Know!

1. Write one or two sentences using as many of the words in the EAD and ED letter patterns as you can.

2. The teacher or another student will dictate each of these six words for you to write without looking at this page. Use each word in a sentence when it is spoken.

bred	**head**	**sled**	**read**	**bread**	**fed**

54 band vs. banned

band = A group that plays music. *"The <u>band</u> was playing rock music."* (n.)

A group. *"There was a <u>band</u> of thieves."* (n.)

banned = Not allowed. *"They were <u>banned</u> from the playground."* (v.)

1. The noisy students were _____ from the library.
2. My favorite _____ is playing at a local club tonight.
3. That _____ of men looks dangerous.
4. I didn't do my homework, so my mother _____ me from the home computer for one month.

Phonics: Short A

Learn to spell all the words in bold print.

Pay attention to the same vowel letter pattern in each word.

The Short A sound is made in the AND letter pattern.

band	**hand**	**land**	**sand**
brand	**gland**	**stand**	**strand**

The Short A sound is also made in the ANNED letter pattern.

banned	**canned**	**fanned**	**tanned**
planned	**scanned**	**panned**	**spanned**

Show YOU Know!

1. Write one or two sentences using as many of the words in the AND and ANNED letter patterns as you can.

2. The teacher or another student will dictate each of these six words for you to write without looking at this page. Use each word in a sentence when it is spoken.

band   scanned   brand   planned   banned   hand

root = The part of a plant that grows in the ground. *"The root collects water and food for the plant."* (n.)

To cheer for someone or something. *"I always root for my school team."* (v.)

route = A certain way to travel from one place to another. *"You can follow Route 6 all the way to the next town."* (n.)

Which Is Right?

1. The orange part of the carrot is the _____ of the plant.

2. That path is the best _____ to the church.

3. His friends like to _____ for the soccer player.

4. You need to decide on a _____ to take from home to school.

Phonics: Short OO

Learn to spell all the words in bold print. Pay attention to the same vowel letter pattern in each word.

The Short OO sound is made in the OOT letter pattern.

root	**boot**	**loot**	**toot**
shoot	**scoot**	**moot**	**hoot**

The Short OO sound is also made by the OUTE letter pattern in only one word.

route

This sound is usually spelled UTE, as in:

flute   **mute**   **brute**

Show YOU Know!

1. Write one or two sentences using as many of the words in the OOT and OUTE letter patterns as you can.

2. The teacher or another student will dictate each of these six words for you to write without looking at this page. Use each word in a sentence when it is spoken.

root   hoot   shoot   boot   route   scoot

56 peak vs. peek

peak = The pointed top of a hill or mountain. *"They climbed up to the peak of the mountain."* (n.)

The highest level of something. *"Not many ball players retire at the peak of their careers."* (n.)

peek = To take a quick, secret look. *"Cover you eyes and don't peek!"* (v.)

Which Is Right?

1. We had a picnic on the _____ of that hill.
2. Becoming president was the _____ of his work at the company.
3. You shouldn't _____ at your present before your birthday.
4. Don't _____ at the book during the quiz.

Phonics: Long E

Learn to spell all the words in bold print.
Pay attention to the same vowel letter pattern in each word.
The Long E sound is made in the EAK letter pattern.

peak	**leak**	**tweak**	**squeak**
sneak	**bleak**	**creak**	**weak**

The Long E sound is also made by the EEK letter pattern.

peek	**reek**	**leek**	**week**
sleek	**cheek**	**Greek**	**seek**

Show YOU Know!

1. Write one or two sentences using as many of the words in the EAK and EEK letter patterns as you can.
2. The teacher or another student will dictate each of these six words for you to write without looking at this page. Use each word in a sentence when it is spoken.

peek   **seek**   **peak**   **sneak**   **week**   **squeak**

57 one vs. won

one = The first number. *"One comes before two."* (n.)

A single person or thing. *"One more can sit at this table."* (n.)

won = Having success over someone or something else. *"If you finish first, you will have won the race."* (v.)

Which Is Right?

1. My team _____ the first game of the season.

2. Please count to twenty beginning with _____.

3. The great swimmer _____ many gold medals at the Olympics.

4. History is the _____ class I really love.

Phonics: Short U

Learn to spell all the words in bold print.
Pay attention to the same vowel letter pattern in each word.
The Short U sound is made in the ONE letter pattern.

one   **done**   **none**

The Short U sound is also made in the ON letter pattern.

won   **ton**   **son**

Note that the Beginning Sound in the word "one" is spelled O and makes the phoneme /w/. This occurs only in this word:

one

Show YOU Know!

1. Write one or two sentences using as many of the words in the ONE and ON letter patterns as you can.

2. The teacher or another student will dictate each of these six words for you to write without looking at this page. Use each word in a sentence when it is spoken.

one   **none**   **son**   **ton**   **won**   **done**

58 night vs. knight

night = The dark time between evening and morning. *"You should be home before it gets dark at <u>night</u>."* (n.)

knight = A soldier or nobleman during the Middle Ages. *"This story is about a <u>knight</u> in King Arthur's court."* (n.)

Which Is Right?

1. It must have been exciting to be a _____ during the Middle Ages.
2. I watched a funny show on television last _____.
3. That actor will play a _____ in his next movie.
4. I go to sleep every _____ at the same time.

Phonics: Long I

Learn to spell all the words in bold print.
Pay attention to the same vowel letter pattern in each word.
The Long I sound is made in the IGHT letter pattern.

knight	**night**	**might**	**sight**
blight	**bright**	**flight**	**slight**

Note that the Beginning Sound in the word "write" is spelled WR and makes the phoneme /r/, as in:

write	**wrong**	**wrote**	**wring**

The letter W in front of the letter R is silent.

Show YOU Know!

1. Write one or two sentences using as many of the words in the IGHT letter pattern as you can.
2. The teacher or another student will dictate each of these six words for you to write without looking at this page. Use each word in a sentence when it is spoken.

knight   **flight**   **night**   **sight**   **might**   **bright**

59 rose vs. rows

rose = A flower with thorns on its stem. *"This rose is a wonderful shade of red."* (n.)

Past tense of the word "rise." *"They rose from the table at the end of the meeting."* (v.)

rows = Plural of row. *"There were rows of people lined up to buy tickets."* (n.)

Which Is Right?

1. There were _____ of empty seats in the stadium.
2. The yellow _____ is the state flower of Texas.
3. The class _____ from their seats to sing the national anthem.
4. The smoke _____ up the chimney.

Phonics: Long O

Learn to spell all the words in bold print.
Pay attention to the same vowel letter pattern in each word.
The Long O sound is made in the OSE letter pattern.

rose	nose	hose	pose
chose	close	prose	those

The Long O sound is also made in the OWS letter pattern.

rows	knows	lows	blows
crows	glows	grows	shows

Show YOU Know!

1. Write one or two sentences using as many of the words in the OSE and OWS letter patterns as you can.
2. The teacher or another student will dictate each of these six words for you to write without looking at this page. Use each word in a sentence when it is spoken.

rose   those   grows   shows   rows   nose

60 pail vs. pale

pail = A container with a handle, usually used for carrying liquid. *"Jack and Jill used a pail to carry water."* (n.)

pale = Something that doesn't have much color. *"The man with the flu looked pale."* (adj.)

Which Is Right?

1. This light blue paint is too _____.

2. I can use a _____ to empty out the flooded boat.

3. I want to fill that _____ with mud.

4. My sister wants to get a suntan so she won't look so _____.

Phonics: Long A

Learn to spell all the words in bold print.

Pay attention to the same vowel letter pattern in each word.

The Long A sound is made by the AIL letter pattern.

pail	**sail**	**nail**	**jail**
hail	**Gail**	**fail**	**bail**

The Long A sound is also made by the ALE letter pattern.

pale	**shale**	**dale**
sale	**male**	**scale**

Show YOU Know!

1. Write one or two sentences using as many of the words in the AIL and ALE letter patterns as you can.

2. The teacher or another student will dictate each of these six words for you to write without looking at this page. Use each word in a sentence when it is spoken.

pale	**jail**	**sale**	**pail**	**male**	**fail**

in = Within. *"Please come in."* (prep.)

inn = A small hotel. *"We will spend the night at the cozy inn."* (n.)

Which Is Right?

1. We need to be _____ the classroom in five minutes.

2. They're building an _____ near the restaurant.

3. That small _____ has only eight rooms.

4. Will you please put the pencils _____ that box?

Phonics: Short I

Learn to spell all the words in bold print.

Pay attention to the same vowel letter pattern in each word.

The Short I sound is made in the IN letter pattern.

in	**pin**	**tin**	**win**
fin	**chin**	**skin**	**thin**

The Short I sound is also made by the INN letter pattern only in one word.

inn

Show YOU Know!

1. Write one or two sentences using as many of the words in the IN and INN letter patterns as you can.

2. The teacher or another student will dictate each of these six words for you to write without looking at this page. Use each word in a sentence when it is spoken.

in   **win**   **thin**   **chin**   **inn**   **fin**

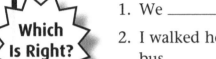

road = An open space that's used for travel. *"I'll get to school if I stay on this road."* (n.)

rode = Past tense of "ride." *"The cowboy rode a wild horse in the rodeo."* (v.)

Which Is Right?

1. We _____ in the car all the way to the mountains.
2. I walked home from the movies, but my friend _____ the bus.
3. This _____ is lined with trees.
4. Our trip will be faster if we take the new _____.

Phonics: Long O

Learn to spell all the words in bold print.

Pay attention to the same vowel letter pattern in each word.

The Long O sound is made in the OAD letter pattern.

road   load   toad   goad

The Long O sound is also made in the ODE letter pattern.

rode   code   strode   mode

Show YOU Know!

1. Write one or two sentences using as many of the words in the ODE and OAD letter patterns as you can.

2. The teacher or another student will dictate each of these six words for you to write without looking at this page. Use each word in a sentence when it is spoken.

road   toad   rode   code   mode   load

64

pair = Two of anything that are used together. *"I like this pair of shoes."* (n.)

pear = A rounded, sweet fruit. *"I'd love to have a pear with my lunch."* (n.)

Which Is Right?

1. I have a _____ of mittens that I wear in the winter.

2. I'm giving my mother a _____ of earrings for her birthday.

3. Can you reach high enough to pick that _____ in the tree?

4. I have enough money to buy two apples and a _____.

Phonics: /e(∂)/

Learn to spell all the words in bold print.

Pay attention to the same vowel letter pattern in each word.

The /e(∂)/ sound is made by the AIR letter pattern.

> **pair   hair   lair   chair**
> **flair   stair   air**

The /e(∂)/ sound is also made by the EA(R) letter pattern.

> **pear   bear   tear   wear   swear**

Show YOU Know!

1. Write one or two sentences using as many of the words in the AIR and EAR letter patterns as you can.

2. The teacher or another student will dictate each of these six words for you to write without looking at this page. Use each word in a sentence when it is spoken.

> **pear   chair   hair   wear   pair   bear**

64 him vs. hymn

him = Referring to a male. *"I like him."* (pron.)

hymn = A song that praises God. *"We sang a hymn at church."* (n.)

Which Is Right?

1. I want to vote for _____.

2. Please ask _____ to come into the room.

3. I like this _____ that we sing each Sunday.

4. We will sing a _____ at the end of the church service.

Phonics: Short I

Learn to spell all the words in bold print.

Pay attention to the same vowel letter pattern in each word.

The Short I sound is made in the IM letter pattern.

him	**skim**	**swim**	**trim**
rim	**dim**	**brim**	**vim**

The Short I sound is also made by the YMN letter pattern in only one word.

hymn

Show YOU Know!

1. Write one or two sentences using as many of the words in the IM and YMN letter patterns as you can.

2. The teacher or another student will dictate each of these six words for you to write without looking at this page. Use each word in a sentence when it is spoken.

him   trim   rim   swim   hymn   skim

fur = The coat of an animal. *"My cat's fur is matted."* (n.)

fir = An evergreen tree. *"We have a fir tree in the front yard."* (n.)

Which Is Right?

1. That hill is covered with _____ trees.

2. My mother used to own a _____ coat.

3. My dog has soft brown _____.

4. That _____ tree has long needles.

Phonics: Short U

Learn to spell all the words in bold print.

Pay attention to the same vowel letter pattern in each word.

The Short U sound is made in the UR letter pattern.

fur   **cur**   **blur**   **spur**

The Short U sound is also made in the IR letter pattern.

fir   **sir**   **stir**   **whir**

Show YOU Know!

1. Write one or two sentences using as many of the words in the IR and UR letter patterns as you can.

2. The teacher or another student will dictate each of these six words for you to write without looking at this page. Use each word in a sentence when it is spoken.

fir   sir   spur   fir   blur   stir

66 hair vs. hare

hair = Thin strands that cover the skin. *"She brushes her <u>hair</u> every day."* (n.)

hare = An animal with long ears and long back legs for jumping. *"I love the story of the tortoise and the <u>hare</u>."* (n.)

Which Is Right?

1. A small _____ is also called a rabbit.

2. I'm going to brush my _____ into a ponytail.

3. I think my pet _____ can jump farther than yours.

4. Her _____ has grown longer than mine.

Phonics: Long A

Learn to spell all the words in bold print.

Pay attention to the same vowel letter pattern in each word.

The Long A sound is made in the AIR letter pattern.

hair	**chair**	**fair**	**pair**
flair	**glair**	**stair**	**fair**

The Long A sound is also made in the ARE letter pattern.

hare	**bare**	**mare**	**rare**
share	**square**	**spare**	**scare**

Show YOU Know!

1. Write one or two sentences using as many of the words in the AIR and ARE letter patterns as you can.

2. The teacher or another student will dictate each of these six words for you to write without looking at this page. Use each word in a sentence when it is spoken.

hare	**scare**	**pair**	**fair**	**hair**	**rare**

67 new vs. knew

new = Something that never existed before. *"These shiny boots are <u>new</u>."* (adj.)

knew = Past tense of "know." *"I <u>knew</u> all the answers on the test."* (v.)

Which Is Right?

1. I _____ you would be here when I got home.
2. She _____ the best way to drive to the restaurant.
3. Many of the buildings in this town are _____.
4. May I buy a _____ dress at the store?

Phonics: Long OO

Learn to spell all the words in bold print.

Pay attention to the same vowel letter pattern in each word.

The Long OO sound is made by the EW letter pattern.

new	**knew**	**few**	**dew**
blew	**chew**	**flew**	**crew**

Note that the Beginning Sound in the word "knew" is spelled KN and makes the phoneme /n/ as in:

knew	**know**	**knight**	**knee**
knife	**knot**	**knock**	**knob**

Show YOU Know!

1. Write one or two sentences using as many of the words in the EW and KN letter patterns as you can.

2. The teacher or another student will dictate each of these six words for you to write without looking at this page. Use each word in a sentence when it is spoken.

new	**crew**	**blew**	**chew**	**knew**	**dew**

68 higher vs. hire

higher = Something above someone or something else. *"I'll be sitting higher in the balcony than you."* (adj.)

hire = To pay someone for work. *"We need to hire more people for this job."* (v.)

Which Is Right?

1. The balloon is floating _____ into the clouds.
2. Will they _____ a lot of people at the new hotel?
3. I'll have to _____ some people to help me move.
4. I'm going to move to a new office that's _____ in this building.

Phonics: Long I

Learn to spell all the words in bold print.

Pay attention to the same vowel letter pattern in each word.

The Long I sound is made in the IGHER letter pattern in only one word.

higher

The Long I sound is also made by the IRE letter pattern.

hire	**fire**	**tire**	**wire**
spire	**quire**	**dire**	**sire**

Show YOU Know!

1. Write one or two sentences using as many of the words in the IGHER and IRE letter patterns as you can.

2. The teacher or another student will dictate each of these six words for you to write without looking at this page. Use each word in a sentence when it is spoken.

hire   tire   wire   higher   fire   spire

69 flu vs. flew

flu = An illness that causes fever, aches, and an upset stomach. *"The winter is often the time when people get the flu."* (n.)

flew = Did fly. Past tense of "fly." *"The bird flew up into the tree."* (v.)

Which Is Right?

1. That airplane _____ to New York City without stopping.
2. I hope I will be healthy and not get the _____ this year.
3. I always get a high fever when I have the _____.
4. A bee _____ in the window and surprised me!

Phonics: Long OO

Learn to spell all the words in bold print.

Pay attention to the same vowel letter pattern in each word.

The Long OO sound is made by the U letter pattern in only one common word.

flu

The Long OO sound is also made by the EW letter pattern.

flew	**dew**	**few**	**knew**
new	**pew**	**yew**	**Jew**

Show YOU Know!

1. Write one or two sentences using as many of the words in the U and EW letter patterns as you can.

2. The teacher or another student will dictate each of these six words for you to write without looking at this page. Use each word in a sentence when it is spoken.

flew   few   flu   new   knew   dew

70 great vs. grate

great = Big in size or number. *"We have a great oak tree in our yard."* (adj.)

Anything that is outstanding. *"The food at our holiday celebration was great."* (adj.)

grate = To rub something against a rough surface to make smaller pieces. *"I want to grate some cheese for this spaghetti."* (v.)

A harsh sound. *"That sound can really grate on my nerves!"* (v.)

Which Is Right?

1. My dance class has a _____ number of students.
2. If you _____ some chocolate, we can sprinkle it on ice cream.
3. I think our new sports stadium is _____!
4. The sound of the jack hammer can _____ after a few minutes.

Phonics: Long A

Learn to spell all the words in bold print.
Pay attention to the same vowel letter pattern in each word.
The Long A sound is made in the EAT letter pattern in only one word.

great

The Long A sound is also made by the ATE letter pattern.

grate	**date**	**gate**	**hate**
rate	**mate**	**late**	**Kate**

Show YOU Know!

1. Write one or two sentences using as many of the words in the EAT and ATE letter patterns as you can.

2. The teacher or another student will dictate each of these six words for you to write without looking at this page. Use each word in a sentence when it is spoken.

great	**gate**	**late**	**date**	**grate**	**rate**

71 hi vs. high

hi = A casual way to say hello. *"She always says 'hi' when I see her."* (interj.)

high = Something of more than usual height. *"They want to build a very high building right in the middle of our town."* (adj.)

Which Is Right?

1. "_____, how are you?"
2. That window washer is working _____ on the building.
3. It's polite to say "hello" or "_____" when you see someone you know.
4. Those birds are flying _____ in the sky.

Phonics: Long I

Learn to spell all the words in bold print.
Pay attention to the same vowel letter pattern in each word.
The Long I sound is made in the IGH letter pattern.

high   **sigh**   **thigh**

The Long I sound is also made by the I letter pattern.

hi   **I**

The Long I sound is usually spelled Y, as in:

sky   **cry**   **buy**   **by**

Show YOU Know!

1. Write one or two sentences using as many of the words in the IGH and I letter patterns as you can.
2. The teacher or another student will dictate each of these five words for you to write without looking at this page. Use each word in a sentence when it is spoken.

hi   **sigh**   **I**   **thigh**   **high**

find = To look for and come upon. *"I hope I find some buried treasure."* (v.)

fined = To make someone pay for breaking a law. *"He was fined $100 for littering."* (v.)

1. Can you help me _____ my glasses?

2. The careless driver was _____ for speeding.

3. That man who crossed the street was _____ for jaywalking.

4. I want to _____ shoes to match this dress.

Phonics: Long I

Learn to spell all the words in bold print.

Pay attention to the same vowel letter pattern in each word.

The Long I sound is made in the IND letter pattern.

find	**kind**	**mind**	**wind**
bind	**hind**	**blind**	**grind**

The Long I sound is also made by the INED letter pattern.

fined	**lined**	**shined**	**pined**

Show YOU Know!

1. Write one or two sentences using as many of the words in the IND and INED letter patterns as you can.

2. The teacher or another student will dictate each of these six words for you to write without looking at this page. Use each word in a sentence when it is spoken.

find	**kind**	**blind**	**wind**	**grind**	**fined**

73 so vs. sew

so = In that way, in the way shown. *"You need to study <u>so</u> you can pass the test."* (adv.)

sew = Using a thread and needle to make or mend. *"I need to <u>sew</u> a button on your shirt."* (v.)

Which Is Right?

1. You need to go by the library ____ you can take out a book.
2. My mother said she would ____ a new dress for me for the dance.
3. I can ____ that ripped sleeve for you.
4. Eat a good breakfast ____ you can play well at the game.

Phonics: Long O

Learn to spell all the words in bold print.
Pay attention to the same vowel letter pattern in each word.
The Long O sound is made by the O letter pattern.

> **so**　　　**no**　　　**go**　　　**pro**

The Long O sound is also made by the EW letter pattern in only one word.

> **sew**

The Long O sound at the end of a word is more often spelled OW, as in:

> **grow**　　　**low**　　　**show**　　　**snow**

Show YOU Know!

1. Write one or two sentences using as many of the words in the O, EW, and OW letter patterns as you can.
2. The teacher or another student will dictate each of these six words for you to write without looking at this page. Use each word in a sentence when it is spoken.

> **sew**　　　**go**　　　**pro**　　　**no**　　　**so**　　　**snow**

raise = To move or lift something to a higher position. *"Please raise your hand before asking a question."* (v.)

To increase the size or amount of something. *"I'm going to raise your allowance next month."* (v.)

rays = A line or beam of heat or light. *"Flowers need rays of sunlight to grow."* (n.)

A thin line coming out from a center. *"The petals of a daisy and the arms of a starfish are rays."* (n.)

Which Is Right?

1. Which student would like to _____ the flag today?
2. The metal spokes of the bicycle wheel are _____.
3. The crew will _____ the sunken ship.
4. I can feel the _____ of the sun hitting my face.

Phonics: Long A

Learn to spell all the words in bold print.
Pay attention to the same vowel letter pattern in each word.
The Long A sound is made in the AISE letter pattern.

raise　　　　　**praise**　　　　　**chaise**

The Long A sound is also made in the AYS letter pattern.

rays　　　　　**days**　　　　　**bays**

Show YOU Know!

1. Write one or two sentences using as many of the words in the AISE and AYS letter patterns as you can.
2. The teacher or another student will dictate each of these six words for you to write without looking at this page. Use each word in a sentence when it is spoken.

raise　　**bays**　　**rays**　　**days**　　**praise**　　**chaise**

way = How a task is completed. *"I found a new way to make a smoothie!"* (n.)

How to travel from place to place. *"Is this the way to your house?"* (n.)

weigh = Finding out the weight of something. *"You have to weigh this box before you mail it."* (v.)

Which Is Right?

1. Is this the fastest _____ to go to the grocery store?

2. I can use these scales to _____ myself in the morning.

3. How much do you think that big dictionary would _____?

4. I'm going to find a new _____ to fix my hair.

Phonics: Long A

Learn to spell all the words in bold print.

Pay attention to the same vowel letter pattern in each word.

The Long A sound is made by the AY letter pattern.

way	**say**	**play**
clay	**gray**	**pray**

The Long A sound is also made by the EI letter pattern.

weigh   **sleigh**

Show YOU Know!

1. Write one or two sentences using as many of the words in the AY and EI letter patterns as you can.

2. The teacher or another student will dictate each of these six words for you to write without looking at this page. Use each word in a sentence when it is spoken.

weigh   **play**   **gray**   **clay**   **way**   **sleigh**

76 ant vs. aunt

ant = A small crawling insect that lives in a colony. *"I see an <u>ant</u> on the kitchen counter!"* (n.)

aunt = Father's or mother's sister or sister-in-law. *"My <u>Aunt</u> Kim came to visit me yesterday."* (n.)

Which Is Right?

1. When you see one _____, there are usually more to be found.
2. I hope I don't see one _____ at our picnic.
3. Will your _____ be coming to your graduation?
4. My _____ and uncle live on a large farm in Kansas.

Phonics: Short A

Learn to spell all the words in bold print.

Pay attention to the same vowel letter pattern in each word.

The Short A sound is made in the ANT letter pattern.

ant	**can't**	**plant**
slant	**chant**	**grant**

The Short A sound is also made by the U letter pattern, only in one word.

aunt

Show YOU Know!

1. Write one or two sentences using as many of the words in the ANT and U letter patterns as you can.

2. The teacher or another student will dictate each of these six words for you to write without looking at this page. Use each word in a sentence when it is spoken.

ant   chant   plant   aunt   slant   can't

77 berry vs. bury

berry = Small, juicy fruits, such as strawberries or blueberries. *"The <u>berry</u> pie was delicious."* (n.)

bury = To dig or make a hole, put something in it, then cover it up. *"My dog likes to <u>bury</u> her bones in the backyard."* (v.)

Which Is Right?

1. I love to drink a _____ smoothie for breakfast.

2. I can't fit one more _____ in my basket!

3. If you _____ that important paper in that pile on your desk, you'll never find it.

4. The town is going to _____ a time capsule near the capitol building.

Phonics: /er/ sound

Learn to spell all the words in bold print.

Pay attention to the same vowel letter pattern in each word.

The /er/ sound is made by the URY letter pattern in only one word.

bury

The /er/ sound is also made by the ERRY letter pattern.

berry	**cherry**	**merry**
ferry	**Sherry**	**Jerry**

Show YOU Know!

1. Write one or two sentences using as many of the words in the URY and ERRY letter patterns as you can.

2. The teacher or another student will dictate each of these six words for you to write without looking at this page. Use each word in a sentence when it is spoken.

berry   cherry   merry   bury   ferry   Jerry

78 blue vs. blew

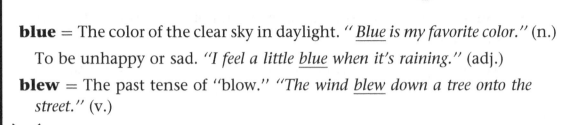

blue = The color of the clear sky in daylight. *"Blue is my favorite color."* (n.)

To be unhappy or sad. *"I feel a little blue when it's raining."* (adj.)

blew = The past tense of "blow." *"The wind blew down a tree onto the street."* (v.)

Which Is Right?

1. In the story, the Big Bad Wolf _____ down the house made of straw.

2. I'm going to paint the walls of my room a pale _____.

3. She _____ out all the candles on her birthday cake.

4. If you add green to _____, you get turquoise.

Phonics: Long OO

Learn to spell all the words in bold print. .
Pay attention to the same vowel letter pattern in each word.
The Long OO sound is made by the UE letter pattern.

blue	**due**	**glue**
true	**clue**	**hue**

The Long OO sound is also made by the EW letter pattern.

blew	**few**	**knew**
new	**threw**	**stew**

Show YOU Know!

1. Write one or two sentences using as many of the words in the UE and EW letter patterns as you can.

2. The teacher or another student will dictate each of these six words for you to write without looking at this page. Use each word in a sentence when it is spoken.

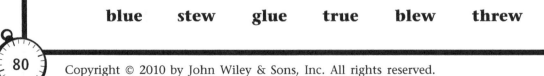

blue   stew   glue   true   blew   threw

our = Belonging to us. *"The trip to Hawaii was <u>our</u> favorite vacation."* (adj.)

hour = Sixty minutes. *"This class lasts almost one <u>hour</u>."* (n.)

Which Is Right?

1. It takes almost an _____ to get to my grandfather's house.

2. _____ garden is beautiful this year.

3. The last book we read in class was _____ favorite one this year.

4. That television show lasts for one _____.

Phonics: /our/ sound

Learn to spell all the words in bold print.

Pay attention to the same vowel letter pattern in each word.

The /our/ sound is made by the OUR letter pattern.

hour   **sour**   **flour**   **our**

Note that the Beginning Sound in the word "hour" is spelled H and is silent, as in:

hour   **honest**   **honor**

Show YOU Know!

1. Write one or two sentences using as many of the words in the OUR letter pattern as you can.

2. The teacher or another student will dictate each of these six words for you to write without looking at this page. Use each word in a sentence when it is spoken.

hour   **flour**   **honor**   **sour**   **our**   **honest**

80 plum vs. plumb

plum = A small purple fruit that has one large seed. *"I'd like to eat that plum with my lunch."* (n.)

plumb = A small weight hung on the end of a line—used to test the depth of water or to find out if a wall is vertical. *"The plumb was tied to the line and dropped into the lake."* (n.)

Which Is Right?

1. The _____ showed that the shoreline was too shallow for the boat to land.

2. That _____ was sweet and juicy.

3. You may pick a _____ from that tree, if you would like.

4. You need to test the strength of the line with the _____ attached to it, to make sure it won't break.

Phonics: Short U

Learn to spell all the words in bold print.

Pay attention to the same vowel letter pattern in each word.

The Short U sound is made by the UM letter pattern.

plum	**gum**	**sum**
chum	**drum**	**glum**

The Short U sound is also made by the UMB letter pattern.

plumb	**dumb**	**crumb**	**thumb**

Show YOU Know!

1. Write one or two sentences using as many of the words in the UM and UMB letter patterns as you can.

2. The teacher or another student will dictate each of these six words for you to write without looking at this page. Use each word in a sentence when it is spoken.

plumb	**dumb**	**sum**	**drum**	**thumb**	**plum**

81 read vs. reed

read = To get the meaning of writing or print. *"My mother likes to read the newspaper every day."* (v.)

To say aloud the words you see. *"I wish you would read that story to me again."* (v.)

reed = Tall grass that grows in wet areas. *"The reed is so thick in this area, it's hard to see the water."* (n.)

A thin strip of wood in the mouthpiece of an instrument that makes sound when you blow air by it. *"My sister has a new reed for her saxophone."* (n.)

Which Is Right?

1. If you _____ a bedtime story to my little brother, he goes right to sleep.

2. I'm going to the music shop to buy a _____ for my clarinet.

3. I'm going to _____ my favorite book again.

4. Be careful! The _____ is thick by the lake, and it's hard to walk.

Phonics: Long E

Learn to spell all the words in bold print. Pay attention to the same vowel letter pattern in each word.

The Long E sound is made by the EAD letter pattern.

read   **bead**   **lead**   **plead**

The Long E sound is also made by the EED letter pattern.

reed   **weed**   **feed**   **need**   **seed**   **deed**

Show YOU Know!

1. Write one or two sentences using as many of the words in the EAD and EED letter patterns as you can.

2. The teacher or another student will dictate each of these six words for you to write without looking at this page. Use each word in a sentence when it is spoken.

read   lead   feed   need   reed   bead

82 ring vs. wring

ring = A circle. *"We always stand in a <u>ring</u> when we begin class."* (n.)

A small band of metal worn on the finger. *"My aunt has a beautiful engagement <u>ring</u>."* (n.)

wring = To twist or squeeze hard. *"Please help me <u>wring</u> out these wet towels."* (v.)

Which Is Right?

1. It's nice to sit in a _____ around the campfire.
2. Please _____ out the dishtowel before you use it again.
3. I have a diamond _____ that belonged to my grandmother.
4. When we go camping, we _____ out the laundry and hang it on the line.

Phonics: Short I

Learn to spell all the words in bold print.
Pay attention to the same vowel letter pattern in each word.
The Short I sound is made in the ING letter pattern.

ring	**wring**	**sing**
string	**bring**	**thing**

Note that the Beginning Sound in the word "wring" is spelled WR and makes the phoneme /r/ as in:

wring	**write**	**wrong**
wreck	**wrench**	**wrap**

Show YOU Know!

1. Write one or two sentences using as many of the words in the ING letter pattern as you can.
2. The teacher or another student will dictate each of these six words for you to write without looking at this page. Use each word in a sentence when it is spoken.

ring   thing   write   wring   wrap   string

toe = One of the five divided areas at the end of the foot. *"I have a blister on my little toe."* (n.)

tow = Pulling something, often with a rope or chain. *"The only way to move that old car is to tow it away."* (v.)

Which Is Right?

1. We have to _____ away the tree that fell down in our yard.
2. A truck will be coming to _____ my car because the battery died.
3. I love to walk near the ocean and feel the sand between my _____.
4. While playing soccer, I hurt my big _____.

Phonics: Long O

Learn to spell all the words in bold print.
Pay attention to the same vowel letter pattern in each word.
The Long O sound is made by the OE letter pattern.

toe	**doe**	**Joe**
hoe	**foe**	**woe**

The Long O sound is also made by the OW letter pattern.

tow	**row**	**mow**
sow	**know**	**grow**

Show YOU Know!

1. Write one or two sentences using as many of the words in the OE and OW letter patterns as you can.
2. The teacher or another student will dictate each of these six words for you to write without looking at this page. Use each word in a sentence when it is spoken.

tow	**foe**	**mow**	**grow**	**toe**	**doe**

rap = To hit sharply. *"I heard someone rap on the door."* (v.)

Music where the vocalist talks in rhythm instead of singing. *"Many young people today listen to rap music."* (n.)

wrap = To cover or conceal something. *"It took me a long time to wrap your birthday present."* (v.)

Which Is Right?

1. I need to _____ this present before I can go to the party.
2. Sometimes it can be hard to understand the words in _____ music.
3. We should _____ the chair in plastic before we paint the wall.
4. My neighbor will sometimes _____ on my window to get me to come outside.

Phonics: Short A

Learn to spell all the words in bold print.
Pay attention to the same vowel letter pattern in each word.
The Short A sound is made by the AP letter pattern.

rap	**cap**	**map**
slap	**trap**	**sap**

Note that the Beginning Sound in the word "wrap" is spelled WR and makes the phoneme /r/ as in:

wrap	**wreath**	**wriggle**
wren	**written**	**wrinkle**

Show YOU Know!

1. Write one or two sentences using as many of the words in the AP letter pattern as you can.
2. The teacher or another student will dictate each of these six words for you to write without looking at this page. Use each word in a sentence when it is spoken.

wrap   map   wrinkle   slap   rap   written

85 warn vs. worn

warn = To give notice of danger. *"They had to <u>warn</u> the man of a plot against him."* (v.)

worn = Past tense of "wear." *"Those shoes have been <u>worn</u> many times."* (v.)

Damaged by use. *"The <u>worn</u> tires on that car are dangerous."* (<u>adj.</u>)

Which Is Right?

1. We'll _____ you if we see your enemy coming this way.

2. My rain boots are so _____, they don't protect my feet from the water anymore.

3. The signs _____ you not to swim in the dirty water.

4. I have _____ this dress to almost every party this year.

Phonics: /or/ sound

Learn to spell all the words in bold print.

Pay attention to the same vowel letter pattern in each word.

The /or/ sound is made by the OR letter pattern.

worn	**corn**	**horn**
torn	**born**	**thorn**

The /or/ sound is also made by the AR letter pattern in only one word.

warn

Show YOU Know!

1. Write one or two sentences using as many of the words in the OR and AR letter patterns as you can.

2. The teacher or another student will dictate each of these six words for you to write without looking at this page. Use each word in a sentence when it is spoken.

worn   corn   warn   thorn   horn   torn

86 least vs. leased

least = Smallest, or less than any other. *"Please choose the hotel that costs the least amount of money."* (adj.)

leased = Something rented out for a certain length of time. *"We leased a cabin in the mountains for two weeks last summer."* (v.)

Which Is Right?

1. We _____ an apartment on the beach for a week last winter.

2. When I got a new job I _____ a house for a year.

3. They are the _____ likely team to win this year.

4. I think I'll buy the dress that costs the _____.

Phonics: /t/ sound

Learn to spell all the words in bold print.

Pay attention to the same vowel letter pattern in each word.

The /t/ sound is made by the T letter pattern.

least	**beast**	**feast**	**yeast**

The /t/ sound is also made by the ED letter pattern.

leased	**greased**	**creased**

Show YOU Know!

1. Write one or two sentences using as many of the words in the T and ED letter patterns as you can.

2. The teacher or another student will dictate each of these six words for you to write without looking at this page. Use each word in a sentence when it is spoken.

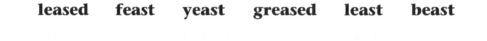

leased	**feast**	**yeast**	**greased**	**least**	**beast**

87 red vs. read

red = A group of colors whose hue is the color of blood. *"I have a <u>red</u> jacket with shoes to match."* (n.)

read = The past tense of "read." *"I <u>read</u> that book and liked it a lot."* (v.)

Which Is Right?

1. My sister's favorite color is _____.
2. I think I'll dye my hair a deep shade of _____.
3. Last year I _____ all seven Harry Potter books again.
4. We _____ a review of that movie in the newspaper.

Phonics: Short E

Learn to spell all the words in bold print.

Pay attention to the same vowel letter pattern in each word.

The Short E sound is made in the ED letter pattern.

red	**bled**	**sled**
Ted	**fed**	**shed**

The Short E sound is also made by the EA letter pattern.

read	**dead**	**thread**
bread	**spread**	**head**

Show YOU Know!

1. Write one or two sentences using as many of the words in the ED and EA letter patterns as you can.

2. The teacher or another student will dictate each of these six words for you to write without looking at this page. Use each word in a sentence when it is spoken.

red	**thread**	**fed**	**read**	**sled**	**spread**

88 bale vs. bail

bale = A large bundle tightly tied for storage or shipping. *"The man worked hard to tie the hay into a bale."* (n.)

bail = The agreement to pay money in return for letting someone out of jail. *"I loaned my cousin the money for his bail when he was arrested for speeding."* (n.)

To throw water out of a boat using a bucket or other container. *"It's hard work to bail water from a sinking boat."* (v.)

Which Is Right?

1. That _____ of grass will be fed to our horses.
2. Please help me _____ out this leaky canoe.
3. The _____ will be very high for the man accused of burglary.
4. That _____ of hay is heavier than it looks!

Phonics: Long A

Learn to spell all the words in bold print.
Pay attention to the same vowel letter pattern in each word.
The Long A sound is made by the A_E letter pattern.

bale	**male**	**tale**
gale	**shale**	**pale**

The Long A sound is also made by the AI letter pattern.

bail	**mail**	**nail**
quail	**rail**	**jail**

Show YOU Know!

1. Write one or two sentences using as many of the words in the A_E and AI letter patterns as you can.
2. The teacher or another student will dictate each of these six words for you to write without looking at this page. Use each word in a sentence when it is spoken.

bail	**tale**	**bale**	**rail**	**mail**	**pale**

89 been vs. bin

been = Past participle of "be." *"This has <u>been</u> a cloudy day."* (v.)

bin = A box used for storage. *"Put your toys in the <u>bin</u>."* (n.)

Which Is Right?

1. The waste _____ is full of recycled bottles and cans.

2. We have _____ hiking for over two hours!

3. It will be easier to clean the _____ when it is empty.

4. The weather has _____ clear and sunny all day.

Phonics: Short I

Learn to spell all the words in bold print.

Pay attention to the same vowel letter pattern in each word.

The Short I sound is made by the I letter pattern.

bin	**fin**	**pin**
win	**din**	**tin**

The Short I sound is also made by the EE letter pattern in only one word.

been

Show YOU Know!

1. Write one or two sentences using as many of the words in the I and EE letter patterns as you can.

2. The teacher or another student will dictate each of these six words for you to write without looking at this page. Use each word in a sentence when it is spoken.

been	**pin**	**tin**	**win**	**bin**	**fin**

90 flower vs. flour

flower = The part of a plant that blooms and makes seeds. *"Our new garden has a type of flower that I've never seen before."* (n.)

To produce flowers. *"The desert cacti flower with beautiful blossoms in the spring."* (v.)

flour = Fine, ground-up wheat or other grains. *"You need to add more flour or the dough will be sticky."* (n.)

To dust or sprinkle with flour. *"Be sure to flour the pan before you pour in the batter."* (v.)

Which Is Right?

1. I'm going to wear a _____ in my hair to the dance tonight.
2. My apron is always covered with _____ after I bake bread.
3. If we're going to make muffins, I'll need to buy more _____ at the grocery store.
4. The gardener will be angry if you pick that _____.

Phonics: /ou/ sound

Learn to spell all the words in bold print.
Pay attention to the same vowel letter pattern in each word.
The /ou/ sound is made by the OW letter pattern.

flower	**power**	**shower**	**tower**

The /ou/ sound is also made by the OU letter pattern.

flour	**hour**	**sour**	**scour**

Show YOU Know!

1. Write one or two sentences using as many of the words in the OW and OU letter patterns as you can.
2. The teacher or another student will dictate each of these six words for you to write without looking at this page. Use each word in a sentence when it is spoken.

flour	**tower**	**sour**	**scour**	**flower**	**power**

PART II

CONTRACTIONS, CAPITALIZATION, COMMON MISSPELLINGS, AND MORE

CONTRACTIONS

Introduction

Contractions take two common words and make them into one word by omitting a letter and replacing it with an apostrophe.

For example: "can not" becomes "can't."

Contractions are often used in writing spoken speech.

For example: She said, "I can't go now."

Contractions are seldom or never used in more formal writing:

For example: "The law says you can not speed."

am

I'm (*I am*)

are

you're (*you are*)
we're
they're
who're

us

let's (*let us*)

is, has

he's (*he is*)
she's
it's
what's

that's
who's
there's
here's
one's
where's
when's
why's
how's

would, had

I'd (*I would, I had*)
you'd
he'd
she'd
we'd

they'd
it'd
there'd
what'd
who'd
that'd
where'd
why'd

have

I've (*I have*)
you've
we've
they've
could've
would've

should've	that'll	shouldn't
might've	these'll	couldn't
who've	those'll	wouldn't
where've	there'll	aren't
when've	this'll	doesn't
must've	what'll	wasn't
will, shall	who'll	weren't
I'll (*I will, I shall*)	where'll	hasn't
you'll	how'll	haven't
she'll	**not**	hadn't
he'll	can't (*can not*)	mustn't
it'll	don't	didn't
we'll	isn't	mightn't
they'll	won't	needn't

Apostrophes are also used in some slang, dialect words, or old-fashioned words.

ain't (am not)　　**d'you** (do you)　　**'tis** (it is)
fo'c'sle (forecastle)　**shan't** (shall not)　**ma'am** (madam)
br'er (dialect for brother)　**y'all** (you all)　**o'clock** (of the clock)
ne'er (never)

91 Contractions: Not

Contractions using "not" are by far the most common.

☞ **DIRECTIONS:** Write out the full two words for these contractions.

Example: *can't = can not*

1. wasn't = _____ _____

2. isn't = _____ _____

3. don't = _____ _____

4. mightn't = _____ _____

5. weren't = _____ _____

6. haven't = _____ _____

☞ **DIRECTIONS:** Now shrink these two words into a contraction.

Example: *has not = hasn't*

7. should not = _____

8. did not = _____

9. could not = _____

10. would not = _____

11. is not = _____

12. can not = _____

92 Contractions: Will or Shall

Contractions using "will" or "shall" end in double l ("ll").

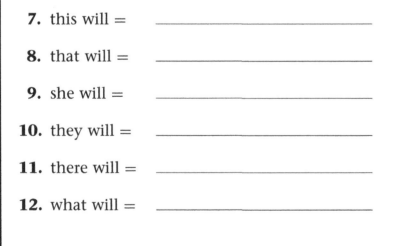 **DIRECTIONS:** Write out the full two words for these contractions.

Example: *they'll = they will*

1. it'll = _____ _____

2. we'll = _____ _____

3. who'll = _____ _____

4. you'll = _____ _____

5. he'll = _____ _____

6. this'll = _____ _____

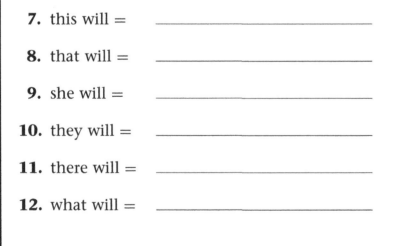 **DIRECTIONS:** Now shrink these two words into a contraction.

Example: *how will = how'll*

7. this will = _____

8. that will = _____

9. she will = _____

10. they will = _____

11. there will = _____

12. what will = _____

98

93 Contractions: Have

Contractions using "have" end in "ve."

☞ **DIRECTIONS:** Write out the full two words for these contractions.

Example: *I've = I have*

1. you've = _____   _____

2. should've = _____   _____

3. who've = _____   _____

4. we've = _____   _____

5. would've = _____   _____

6. must've = _____   _____

☞ **DIRECTIONS:** Now shrink these two words into a contraction.

Example: *we have = we've*

7. they have = _____

8. could have = _____

9. might have = _____

10. I have = _____

11. where have = _____

12. when have = _____

94 Contractions: Would or Had

Contractions using "would" or "had" use only the letter "d."

☞ **DIRECTIONS:** Write out the full two words for these contractions.

Example: *he'd = he would*

1. you'd = _____ _____

2. what'd = _____ _____

3. who'd = _____ _____

4. we'd = _____ _____

5. there'd = _____ _____

6. where'd = _____ _____

☞ **DIRECTIONS:** Now shrink these two words into a contraction.

Example: *we had = we'd*

7. it had = _____

8. they would = _____

9. I had = _____

10. he would = _____

11. she would = _____

12. that had = _____

95 Contractions: Is or Has

Contractions using "is" or "has" add the letter "s."

☞ **DIRECTIONS:** Write out the full two words for these contractions.

Example: why's = why is

1. he's = _____ _____

2. that's = _____ _____

3. here's = _____ _____

4. it's = _____ _____

5. one's = _____ _____

6. where's = _____ _____

☞ **DIRECTIONS:** Now shrink these two words into a contraction.

Example: it has = it's

7. she is = _____

8. what has = _____

9. who is = _____

10. there has = _____

11. when is = _____

12. why is = _____

96 Contractions: Various

☞ **DIRECTIONS:** Write out the full two words for these contractions.

Example: *isn't = is not*

1. you're = _____ _____

2. that'd = _____ _____

3. they're = _____ _____

4. I'm = _____ _____

5. I'll = _____ _____

6. let's = _____ _____

☞ **DIRECTIONS:** Now shrink these two words into a contraction.

Example: *who have = who've*

7. we are = _____

8. who are = _____

9. had not = _____

10. these will = _____

11. can not = _____

12. does not = _____

CAPITALIZATION

Capitalization is definitely a spelling problem. For example, if you write "united states," that is a spelling error.

Lessons 97 through 107 will show you a number of places where the first letter should be capitalized.

There are uses where the same word need not be capitalized. For example:

"He wrote a bad introduction."

And uses where it probably should be capitalized:

"The Introduction is on page 8."

Note that the second use of *introduction* refers to a title.

There are a few words, called Capitonyms, in which capitalization changes the meaning:

Pat is a person's name.

pat is a light tapping.

And a few words in which it changes the pronunciation and meaning:

Polish is a citizen of Poland.

polish is to make shiny.

If you are using spell check on your computer, watch out because it may not correct capitalization errors.

97 Capitalization: First Word

Capitalize the first word in every sentence or question.

Example: *She runs all the time.*

👉 **DIRECTIONS:** Copy the sentences below correctly.

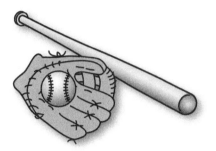

1. the baseball game lasted all day.

_____

2. oil and water do not mix.

_____

3. who was the first president?

_____

4. gorillas like to eat plants.

_____

5. storms begin far out in the ocean.

_____

98 Capitalization: Names

Capitalize names of people.

Example: *William Clinton*

☞ **DIRECTIONS:** Copy the names of the people below correctly.

1. mark twain

_____

2. bill

_____

3. william shakespeare

_____

4. mary smith

_____

5. harry potter

_____

6. carl rodriguez

_____

7. abigail adams

_____

106

99 Capitalization: Places

Capitalize names of places.

Example: *South Africa*

☞ **DIRECTIONS:** Copy the names of the places below correctly.

1. new york

_____

2. los angeles

_____

3. south america

_____

4. michigan

_____

5. pacific ocean

_____

6. italy

_____

7. minneapolis

_____

100 Capitalization: Pets

Capitalize the names of pets.

Example: *Rex*

👉 **DIRECTIONS:** Copy the names of the pets below correctly.

1. spot

_____

2. lassie

_____

3. black beauty

_____

4. king

_____

5. flicka

_____

6. rin tin tin

_____

7. princess

_____

101 Capitalization: Holidays

Capitalize the names of holidays.

Example: *Easter*

☞ **DIRECTIONS:** Copy the names of the holidays below correctly.

1. new year's day

_____

2. fourth of july

_____

3. independence day

_____

4. martin luther king jr. day

_____

5. thanksgiving

_____

Capitalize the first word and main words in titles of books, plays, and movies.

Example: *Black Beauty*

☞ **DIRECTIONS:** Copy the titles of the books below correctly.

1. the adventures of tom sawyer

_____

2. robinson crusoe

_____

3. harry potter and the half-blood prince

_____

4. alice's adventures in wonderland

_____

5. the lord of the rings

_____

6. where the wild things are

_____

103 Capitalization: Periodicals

Capitalize the titles of periodicals.

Example: *Boy's Life*

☞ **DIRECTIONS:** Copy the titles of the periodicals below correctly.

1. reader's digest

_____

2. the los angeles times

_____

3. highlights for children

_____

4. national geographic for kids

_____

5. newsweek

_____

6. the wall street journal

_____

7. teen vogue

_____

104 Capitalization: People's Titles

Capitalize titles of respect.

Example: *Congressman Jones*

☞ **DIRECTIONS:** Copy the titles of respect below correctly.

1. mr. smith

_____

2. ms. smith

_____

3. president washington

_____

4. reverend gonzales

_____

5. senator jones

_____

6. rabbi horowitz

_____

7. sergeant porter

_____

105 Capitalization: Companies

Capitalize names of companies, organizations, and trade names.

Example: *Tinker Toys*

☞ **DIRECTIONS:** Copy the names of companies, organizations, and trade names below correctly.

1. general motors

_____

2. coca-cola

_____

3. boston red sox

_____

4. united states congress

_____

5. methodist church

_____

106 Capitalization: Quotations

Capitalize the first word in a direct quotation.

Example: *The sign said, "No Trespassing!"*

☞ **DIRECTIONS:** Copy the sentences below correctly.

1. Mother asked, "where is the soap?"

_____

2. She yelled, "stop!"

_____

3. The umpire shouted, "play ball!"

_____

4. Bill said, "let's go home."

_____

5. The policeman advised, "you are under arrest."

_____

6. The teacher said, "close your books."

_____

7. Dr. Lewis said, "your arm is broken."

_____

107 Capitalization: Review

☞ **DIRECTIONS:** Circle the words needing capitals.

1. mr. sam malone

2. mrs. jones flew to chicago.

3. my dog, king, came from miami.

4. maria will be home for christmas.

5. have you seen the latest harry potter movie?

6. father likes to read the new york times.

7. the u.s. congress meets in washington.

8. mcdonald's sells millions of big mac hamburgers.

9. the cowboy yelled, "get those animals moving."

10. we went to seattle for the month of april.

COMMON MISSPELLINGS

People who study spelling errors find that certain words tend to be misspelled much more than other words. Lessons 108 to Lesson 117 are some of those words, so pay attention to them when you are writing.

Besides the words in these lessons, you (or any writer) tend to misspell the same word over and over again. You can help this problem by making your own misspelling list so that you pay attention to the words you regularly misspell.

108 Common Misspellings

☞ **DIRECTIONS:** Look at the wrong spelling, then *study* the correct spelling.

Next, write the correct spelling three times.

1. Wrong: **shure**   Correct: **sure**

Write the correct word three times:

_____   _____   _____

Are you *sure*?

2. Wrong: **gard**   Correct: **guard**

Write the correct word three times:

_____   _____   _____

The *guard* is at the door.

3. Wrong: **bigest**   Correct: **biggest**

Write the correct word three times:

_____   _____   _____

I have the *biggest* dog here.

4. Wrong: **Chrismas**   Correct: **Christmas**

Write the correct word three times:

_____   _____   _____

Merry *Christmas*.

5. Wrong: **ofen**   Correct: **often**

Write the correct word three times:

_____   _____   _____

She comes here *often*.

109 Common Misspellings

☞ **DIRECTIONS:** Look at the wrong spelling, then *study* the correct spelling.

Next, write the correct spelling three times.

1. Wrong: **sinse**   Correct: **sin̲ce**

Write the correct word three times:

_____   _____   _____

He has been here *since* Tuesday.

2. Wrong: **oclock**   Correct: **o'clock**

Write the correct word three times:

_____   _____   _____

It is now two *o'clock*.

3. Wrong: **leter**   Correct: **lette̲r**

Write the correct word three times:

_____   _____   _____

Please mail this *letter*.

4. Wrong: **sumer**   Correct: **summ̲er**

Write the correct word three times:

_____   _____   _____

See you next *summer*.

5. Wrong: **frend**   Correct: **fri̲end**

Write the correct word three times:

_____   _____   _____

You are my best *friend*.

110 Common Misspellings

☞ **DIRECTIONS:** Look at the wrong spelling, then *study* the correct spelling.

Next, write the correct spelling three times.

1. Wrong: **wether**   Correct: **we__ather**

Write the correct word three times:

_____   _____   _____

The *weather* is bad.

2. Wrong: **forth**   Correct: **fo__urth**

Write the correct word three times:

_____   _____   _____

The *Fourth* of July is a holiday.

3. Wrong: **wich**   Correct: **w__hich**

Write the correct word three times:

_____   _____   _____

Which one do you like?

4. Wrong: **runing**   Correct: **run__ning**

Write the correct word three times:

_____   _____   _____

The stream is *running*.

5. Wrong: **sene**   Correct: **s__cene**

Write the correct word three times:

_____   _____   _____

She saw a beautiful *scene*.

111 Common Misspellings

☞ **DIRECTIONS:** Look at the wrong spelling, then *study* the correct spelling.

Next, write the correct spelling three times.

1. Wrong: **ment**   Correct: **meant**

Write the correct word three times:

_____   _____   _____

That is what he *meant* to say.

2. Wrong: **hopeing**   Correct: **hoping**

Write the correct word three times:

_____   _____   _____

I was *hoping* you would come.

3. Wrong: **dout**   Correct: **doubt**

Write the correct word three times:

_____   _____   _____

Don't *doubt* it.

4. Wrong: **goverment**   Correct: **government**

Write the correct word three times:

_____   _____   _____

Dad works for the city *government*.

5. Wrong: **ake**   Correct: **ache**

Write the correct word three times:

_____   _____   _____

His back *aches*.

112 Common Misspellings

☞ **DIRECTIONS:** Look at the wrong spelling, then *study* the correct spelling.

Next, write the correct spelling three times.

1. Wrong: **Febuary**   Correct: **Feb_ruary**

Write the correct word three times:

_____   _____   _____

February is the coldest month.

2. Wrong: **anual**   Correct: **an_nual**

Write the correct word three times:

_____   _____   _____

She came for her *annual* visit.

3. Wrong: **neice**   Correct: **n_iece**

Write the correct word three times:

_____   _____   _____

I am her *niece.*

4. Wrong: **similer**   Correct: **simi_lar**

Write the correct word three times:

_____   _____   _____

Both bikes are *similar.*

5. Wrong: **sking**   Correct: **ski_ing**

Write the correct word three times:

_____   _____   _____

We like *skiing.*

113 Common Misspellings

☞ **DIRECTIONS:** Look at the wrong spelling, then *study* the correct spelling.

Next, write the correct spelling three times.

1. Wrong: **truely**   Correct: **truly**

Write the correct word three times:

_____ _____ _____

The letter was signed "Yours *truly*."

2. Wrong: **succes**   Correct: **success**

Write the correct word three times:

_____ _____ _____

We wish you *success*.

3. Wrong: **terribel**   Correct: **terrible**

Write the correct word three times:

_____ _____ _____

Her picture was *terrible*.

4. Wrong: **straght**   Correct: **straight**

Write the correct word three times:

_____ _____ _____

He can't walk *straight*.

5. Wrong: **swiming**   Correct: **swimming**

Write the correct word three times:

_____ _____ _____

Swimming is my best sport.

124

114 Common Misspellings

☞ **DIRECTIONS:** Look at the wrong spelling, then *study* the correct spelling.

Next, write the correct spelling three times.

1. Wrong: **techer**   Correct: **te<u>a</u>cher**

Write the correct word three times:

_____   _____   _____

She is the best *teacher.*

2. Wrong: **Tusday**   Correct: **Tu<u>e</u>sday**

Write the correct word three times:

_____   _____   _____

Be here next *Tuesday.*

3. Wrong: **blu**   Correct: **blu<u>e</u>**

Write the correct word three times:

_____   _____   _____

He has a *blue* shirt.

4. Wrong: **peple**   Correct: **pe<u>o</u>ple**

Write the correct word three times:

_____   _____   _____

Look at all those *people.*

5. Wrong: **prety**   Correct: **pret<u>t</u>y**

Write the correct word three times:

_____   _____   _____

She has a very *pretty* dress.

☞ **DIRECTIONS:** Look at the wrong spelling, then *study* the correct spelling.

Next, write the correct spelling three times.

1. Wrong: **rite**   Correct: **write**

Write the correct word three times:

_____   _____   _____

Write to me soon.

2. Wrong: **tird**   Correct: **tired**

Write the correct word three times:

_____   _____   _____

He looks *tired*.

3. Wrong: **flys**   Correct: **flies**

Write the correct word three times:

_____   _____   _____

There are too many *flies* there.

4. Wrong: **milion**   Correct: **million**

Write the correct word three times:

_____   _____   _____

Give me a *million* dollars.

5. Wrong: **belev**   Correct: **believe**

Write the correct word three times:

_____   _____   _____

I don't *believe* you.

☞ **DIRECTIONS:** Look at the wrong spelling, then *study* the correct spelling.

Next, write the correct spelling three times.

1. Wrong: **nife**   Correct: **knife**

Write the correct word three times:

_____   _____   _____

The *knife* is sharp.

2. Wrong: **libary**   Correct: **library**

Write the correct word three times:

_____   _____   _____

This is a *library* book.

3. Wrong: **aful**   Correct: **awful**

Write the correct word three times:

_____   _____   _____

Lunch was *awful*.

4. Wrong: **arond**   Correct: **around**

Write the correct word three times:

_____   _____   _____

Do you live *around* here?

5. Wrong: **prinsipl**   Correct: **principal**

Write the correct word three times:

_____   _____   _____

The *principal* is great.

117 Common Misspellings

☞ **DIRECTIONS:** Look at the wrong spelling, then *study* the correct spelling.

Next, write the correct spelling three times.

1. Wrong: **saff**   Correct: **safe**

Write the correct word three times:

_____   _____   _____

Is it *safe* to be here?

2. Wrong: **aganst**   Correct: **against**

Write the correct word three times:

_____   _____   _____

Put it *against* the fence.

3. Wrong: **loz**   Correct: **lose**

Write the correct word three times:

_____   _____   _____

I win, you *lose*.

4. Wrong: **foren**   Correct: **foreign**

Write the correct word three times:

_____   _____   _____

This is a *foreign* stamp.

5. Wrong: **crod**   Correct: **crowd**

Write the correct word three times:

_____   _____   _____

The game had a big *crowd*.

PLURALS

Oh, if English spelling were only more consistent, like just adding an S to form a plural. But the last letter in many words determines how the plural is spelled. See Lessons 118 to 126.

There are a few words, called Invariable Nouns, that do not have any change for plurals. For example, *deers* is not a correct spelling. You can have one deer or two deer. (See Lesson 125.)

118 Plurals: For Most Words

The plural form of most nouns is made by adding "-s."

Example: *chair = chairs*

☞ **DIRECTIONS:** Make these nouns into plurals.

president _____   cereal _____

cat _____   desk _____

face _____   rock _____

bowl _____   drill _____

floor _____   hill _____

119 Plurals: For Words Ending in "S" or "SS"

If the word ends in "s" or "ss," the plural is formed by adding "-es."

Examples: *boss = bosses, gas = gases*

☞ **DIRECTIONS:** Make these words plural.

dress _____

loss _____

grass _____

cross _____

bus _____

class _____

moss _____

glass _____

plus _____

class _____

☞ **Note:** Most words ending with the /s/ sound are spelled with a double "ss."

Example: *"dress"*

120 Plurals: For Words Ending in "CH"

If the word ends in "ch," the plural is formed by adding "-es."

Example: *inch = inches*

☞ **DIRECTIONS:** Make these words into plurals.

bench _____

wrench _____

clench _____

pitch _____

watch _____

coach _____

branch _____

touch _____

punch _____

speech _____

121 Plurals: For Words Ending in "SH"

If the word ends in "sh," the plural is formed by adding "-es."

Example: *dish = dishes*

☞ **DIRECTIONS:** Make these words into plurals.

fish   _____

brush   _____

crash   _____

push   _____

wash   _____

squash   _____

smash   _____

clash   _____

ash   _____

flash   _____

122 Plurals: For Words Ending in "X"

If the word ends in "x," the plural is formed by adding "-es."

Example: *fox = foxes*

☞ **DIRECTIONS:** Make these words into plurals.

ax   _____

sex   _____

box   _____

flex   _____

tax   _____

pox   _____

wax   _____

lox   _____

flax   _____

hex   _____

123 Plurals: For Words Ending in "Y"

In most words ending in "y" where the "y" is preceded by a consonant, the plural is spelled by changing the "y" to "i" and adding "-es."

Example: *city = cities*

☞ **DIRECTIONS:** Make these words into plurals.

variety _____

cherry _____

family _____

copy _____

country _____

lady _____

candy _____

army _____

body _____

baby _____

☞ **Note:** Most words (nouns) that end in "y" have a <u>consonant</u> preceding the "y" and follow the rule above. However, a very few nouns ending in "y" have a <u>vowel</u> preceding the "y" and the plural is spelled by just adding an "s."

Examples: *boy = boys, key = keys, play = plays, turkey = turkeys, journey = journeys*

124 Plurals: For Words Ending in "O"

In most words ending in "o" where the "o" is <u>preceded by a consonant,</u> the plural is spelled by adding "-es."

Example: *hero = heroes*

☞ **DIRECTIONS:** Make these words into plurals.

tomato   _____

photo   _____

zero   _____

coco   _____

potato   _____

burro   _____

echo   _____

tobacco   _____

buffalo   _____

veto   _____

☞ **Note:** Most words that end in "o" have a <u>consonant</u> before the "o" and follow the rule above. However, a very few nouns ending in "o" have a <u>vowel</u> before the "o," and the plural is spelled by just adding an "s."

Examples: *radio = radios, video = videos, rodeo = rodeos, studio = studios, patio = patios*

125 Plurals: Irregular Plurals

Some words have irregular plural forms.

Examples:

child to children	ox to oxen
man to men	basis to bases
crisis to crises	index to indices
axis to axes	oasis to oases
die to dice	foot to feet
mouse to mice	radius to radii
tooth to teeth	brother to brethren
woman to women	goose to geese
stimulus to stimuli	medium to media
criterion to criteria	focus to foci
parenthesis to parentheses	datum to data
deer to deer	

☞ **DIRECTIONS:** Using the chart above, write the plural for these words.

tooth _____

ox _____

man _____

goose _____

foot _____

deer _____

child _____

mouse _____

woman _____

index _____

126 Plurals: Invariable Nouns

Some words are used for both singular and plural meanings, and these never use an "-s" or "-es" suffix. These are called <u>invariable nouns</u>.

Examples:

cod	*moose*	*barley*
traffic	*salmon*	*series*
specimen	*deer*	*bass*
mackerel	*dozen*	*hay*
dirt	*music*	*trout*
corps	*rye*	*fish*
sheep	*wheat*	*gross*
Swiss	*British*	*aircraft*

☞ **DIRECTIONS:** Using the list above, write the plural for these words if it is not invariable. If it is invariable, copy the word.

traffic _____

cat _____

moose _____

aircraft _____

British _____

ocean _____

sheep _____

hay _____

wheat _____

dozen _____

music _____

sea _____

ABBREVIATIONS

Introduction

U.S. states always are abbreviated with two capital letters. These are U.S. Post Office official abbreviations, but they are used in many other places, such as Federal Express and UPS. They have largely replaced older and longer state abbreviations, such as "Calif."

STATE CHART

First Two Letters

AL = Alabama

AR = Arkansas

CA = California

CO = Colorado

DE = Delaware

FL = Florida

ID = Idaho

IN = Indiana

MA = Massachusetts

MI = Michigan

NE = Nebraska

OH = Ohio

OK = Oklahoma

OR = Oregon

UT = Utah

WA = Washington

WI = Wisconsin

WY = Wyoming

First and Last Letters

CT = Connecticut

GA = Georgia

HI = Hawaii

IA = Iowa

KS = Kansas

KY = Kentucky

LA = Louisiana

MD = Maryland

ME = Maine

PA = Pennsylvania

VA = Virginia

VT = Vermont

First and Middle Letters

AK = Alaska

AZ = Arizona

MN = Minnesota

MS = Mississippi

MO = Missouri

MT = Montana

NV = Nevada

TN = Tennessee

TX = Texas

Two Words

DC = District of Columbia

NC = North Carolina

ND = North Dakota

NH = New Hampshire

NJ = New Jersey

NM = New Mexico

NY = New York

PR = Puerto Rico

RI = Rhode Island

SC = South Carolina

SD = South Dakota

VI = Virgin Islands

Note: The abbreviation for the "United States" may be "US," "U.S.," "U.S.A.," or "USA."

You can refer to the Abbreviations introduction pages for the correct spelling of the state names.

☞ **DIRECTIONS:** Write out the full spelling for these abbreviations.

1. DE _____

2. MA _____

3. OH _____

4. MI _____

5. WA _____

6. AL _____

7. OK _____

8. FL _____

9. CO _____

10. OR _____

11. CA _____

12. WY _____

13. WI _____

14. UT _____

15. NE _____

16. IN _____

You can refer to the Abbreviations introduction pages for the correct spelling of the state names.

☞ **DIRECTIONS:** Write out the full spelling for these abbreviations.

1. HI _____

2. LA _____

3. VT _____

4. MD _____

5. GA _____

6. KY _____

7. PA _____

8. KS _____

9. CT _____

10. VA _____

11. ME _____

12. IA _____

129 Abbreviations: First and Middle Letters

You can refer to the Abbreviations introduction pages for the correct spelling of the state names.

☞ **DIRECTIONS:** Write out the full spelling for these abbreviations.

1. AZ _____

2. MN _____

3. TX _____

4. MT _____

5. AK _____

6. TN _____

7. NV _____

8. MS _____

9. MO _____

10. TX _____

11. AZ _____

12. NV _____

130 Abbreviations: Two-Word State Names

You can refer to the Abbreviations introduction pages for the correct spelling of the state names.

☞ **DIRECTIONS:** Write out the full spelling for these abbreviations.

1. NH _____

2. WV _____

3. RI _____

4. NY _____

5. SC _____

6. VI _____

7. NM _____

8. SD _____

9. NJ _____

10. PR _____

11. ND _____

12. DC _____

13. NC _____

131 Abbreviations: Initializations

Initializations are a type of abbreviation that uses the first letter of several words. They are usually capitalized and spelled without a period.

PS = Post Script (Additional writing at the end of a letter)

TV = Television

ZIP = Zone Improvement Plan (The numbers used in a postal address)

UN = United Nations

VIP = Very Important Person

RV = Recreational Vehicle

NBC = National Broadcasting Corporation

SUV = Sport Utility Vehicle

UFO = Unidentified Flying Object

PC = Personal Computer

☞ **DIRECTIONS:** Write out the full words for the following initializations.

1. ZIP _____

2. PC _____

3. RV _____

4. UFO _____

5. SUV _____

6. UN _____

7. PS _____

8. NBC _____

9. VIP _____

10. TV _____

What are your initials? _____

132 Abbreviations: Days of the Week

Abbreviations for the days of the week are common and useful. They are most commonly spelled with the first three letters of the word and a period.

Sun. = Sunday

Mon. = Monday

Tue. or Tues. = Tuesday

Wed. or Weds. = Wednesday

Thu. or Thur. or Thurs. = Thursday

Fri. = Friday

Sat. = Saturday

☞ **DIRECTIONS:** Write the three-letter abbreviation for the following words.

1. Friday _____

2. Tuesday _____

3. Saturday _____

4. Monday _____

5. Sunday _____

6. Thursday _____

7. Wednesday _____

133 Abbreviations: Months of the Year

Here are the most used abbreviations for ten months of the year.

Jan. = January

Feb. = February

Mar. = March

Apr. = April

Jul. = July

Aug. = August

Sept. = September

Oct. = October

Nov. = November

Dec. = December

☞ **DIRECTIONS:** Write the abbreviations for each of these months.

1. November _____

2. October _____

3. April _____

4. January _____

5. March _____

6. December _____

7. August _____

8. February _____

9. July _____

10. September _____

134 Abbreviations: Streets

Here are the common abbreviations for streets and roads. These should always be used when writing an address.

Blvd. = Boulevard

Dr. = Drive

St. = Street

Pkwy. = Parkway

Rd. = Road

Hwy. = Highway

Ln. = Lane

Ave. = Avenue

☞ **DIRECTIONS:** Write the common abbreviation for the following words.

1. Street _____

2. Parkway _____

3. Road _____

4. Highway _____

5. Lane _____

6. Boulevard _____

7. Drive _____

8. Avenue _____

☞ **DIRECTIONS:** Write the full word for the following abbreviations.

1. Hwy. _____

2. Dr. _____

3. Ln. _____

4. Blvd. _____

5. Pkwy. _____

6. Rd. _____

7. Ave. _____

8. St. _____

135 Abbreviations: Titles

Here are some common abbreviations for a title of a person. These are nearly always used in writing addresses, but are also commonly used in other writing.

Dr. = Doctor	Mrs. = Mistress
Pres. = President	Capt. = Captain
Supt. = Superintendent	Lt. = Lieutenant
Rev. = Reverend	Sgt. = Sergeant
Mr. = Mister	Prof. = Professor

☞ **DIRECTIONS:** Write the abbreviation for the following titles.

1. Mister   _____

2. Lieutenant   _____

3. Professor   _____

4. President   _____

5. Doctor   _____

6. Superintendent _____

7. Reverend   _____

8. Mistress   _____

9. Mister   _____

10. Sergeant   _____

☞ **Note:** You can use "Ms." for any woman, but "Miss" is used only for a girl or an unmarried woman and is not abbreviated.

136 Abbreviations: Time

Words related to time are frequently abbreviated; television schedules use A.M. and EST, and history books use A.D.

A.M., a.m. = ante meridiem (morning, before noon)
P.M., p.m. = post meridiem (afternoon/evening)
A.D. = Anno Domini (after Christ)
B.C. = Before Christ
hr. = hour
sec. = second
EST = Eastern Standard Time
PST = Pacific Standard Time
mo. = month
wk. = week

☞ **DIRECTIONS:** Write the abbreviation for the following times.

1. Before Christ _____

2. week _____

3. ante meridiem _____

4. second _____

5. Anno Domini _____

6. month _____

7. Eastern Standard Time _____

8. hour _____

9. Pacific Standard Time _____

10. post meridiem _____

☞ **Note:** The periods in some of these abbreviations are sometimes omitted.

In the preceding lessons, there are abbreviations for words in various fields, such as Time, Months, and States. Once you become aware of abbreviations, you will see them used in nearly every field. The list below gives you some different areas that use abbreviations. They are used because they save time and effort for both the reader and the writer (speller).

Airlines (city codes) . . . . LAX = Los Angeles airport
Medical . . . . MS = multiple sclerosis
Government . . . . CIA = Central Intelligence Agency
Measurement . . . . in. = inch
Education . . . . SAT = Scholastic Aptitude Test
Addresses . . . . NY = New York
Names . . . . JFK = John Fitzgerald Kennedy
Books . . . . pg = page
E-mail and Texting . . . . SYL = see you later
Sports . . . . NFL = National Football League

☞ **DIRECTIONS:** Write out the full words for the following abbreviations.

1. MS _____ _____

2. CIA _____ _____ _____

3. in. _____

4. JFK _____ _____ _____

5. NFL _____ _____ _____

6. SAT _____ _____ _____

7. pg _____

8. SYL _____ _____ _____

☞ **Note:** "Clipped words," such as "limo" for "limousine," are often used but are not considered abbreviations.

HOMOPHONE CONTRACTIONS

Contractions mean that one word stands for two words. For example, <u>it's</u> stands for "<u>it is</u>," as in "it's lost."

Spelled without the apostrophe, <u>its</u> is one word, a pronoun that shows possession. For example, "my cat lost its toy."

It's and <u>*its*</u> are homophones because they are pronounced the same but they have different meanings.

155

138 Homophone Contractions: "They're"

Watch out for the spelling of homophones of the contraction "they're."

they're = a <u>contraction</u> of "they are"

    Example: *"They're already home."*

their = a word that shows <u>possession</u>

    Example: *"Students should bring their books."*

there = a word that shows <u>place</u>

    Example: *"It is put over there."*

☞ **Note:** "There" is used in a lot of expressions, such as "There you go" and "There you are."

☞ **DIRECTIONS:** Use the correct homophone in each sentence.

1. _____ not coming.

2. I have never been _____.

3. _____ team might win.

4. What color is _____ flag?

5. It is cool in _____.

6. Do they know where _____ going?

☞ **Note:** Contractions are often used in writing dialogue (spoken words), and contractions are avoided in more formal writing.

139 Homophone Contractions: "You're"

Watch out for the spelling of "you're."

you're = a <u>contraction</u> of "you are"

> **Example:** *"You're not to leave this house."*

your = an adjective that shows <u>possession</u>

> **Example:** *"Where are your books?"*

☞ **DIRECTIONS:** Use the correct homophone in each sentence.

1. I know where _____ going.

2. Do _____ friends know where you are?

3. Where is _____ coat?

4. Now _____ in trouble.

5. _____ not supposed to be there.

6. _____ cap does not fit.

140 Homophone Contractions: "It's"

Watch out for the spelling of the homophone for "it's."

its = a <u>pronoun</u> used in place of a noun; it often refers to a previously used or understood word (shows possession)

   Example: *"Where is its dish?"*

it's = a <u>contraction</u> of "it is"

   Example: *"It's hot today."*

☞ **DIRECTIONS:** Use the correct homophone in each sentence.

1. My dog has lost _____ mind.

2. _____ in the cupboard.

3. _____ color is not good.

4. _____ not what I thought.

5. Where did you put _____ blanket?

6. _____ going to be OK.

141 Homophone Contractions: "Who's"

Watch out for the spelling of the homophone "who's."

who's = the <u>contraction</u> of "who is"

Example: *"Who's going to the show?"*

whose = a word that shows <u>possession</u>

Example: *"Whose car are we taking?"*

☞ **DIRECTIONS:** Use the correct homophone in each sentence.

1. _____ pen is this?

2. I know _____ laughing.

3. _____ the happiest?

4. _____ already finished?

5. _____ shoes are muddy?

6. _____ going to lunch early?

SILENT LETTERS

Introduction

Silent letters are a real spelling problem.

In writing this book, my inclination was to skip them. But several teacher reviewers of the manuscript and my editor said, "Oh, please include something on silent letters." So please excuse this informal and abbreviated essay.

First, it helps to know some phonics if you want to be a good speller, but you need to know much more.

Silent Consonant Digraphs

GN = /n/ (initial)	gnat, gnome, gnarl, gnash
GN =/n/ (final)	sign, design, resign, foreign, reign
KN = /n/ (initial)	know, knee, knife, knot, kneel, knew, knight, knock, knit
WR = /r/	write, writing, wrote, wrist, wreck, wrong, wrench, wring, wrinkle

GH is the so-called Silent Blend, and it occurs in several letter clusters.

AUGHT = /o/	caught, daughter, taught, naughty
EIGH = /a/	sleigh, weigh
IGH = /i/	high, sigh, neighbor, straight
IGHT = /i/	bright, light, night, sight, height
OUGH = /f/	(final) cough, tough, rough, enough
OUGH = /o/	though, although, dough, doughnut
OUGHT = /o/	fought, ought, thought, bought, brought

Silent Letter B

BT = /t/   debt, doubt

MB = /m/   crumb, dumb, thumb, lamb, tomb, climb, bomb, comb, limb, numb

Letter C

silent   The letter C has no sound of its own.

ca, co, cu   C makes the /k/ sound before A, O, and U, as in "cat."

ci, ce, cy   C makes the /s/ sound before I, E, and Y, as in "city."

Silent Letter D

DGE = /j/   badge, wedge, edge, hedge, fudge

Silent Letter E

silent   The letter E at the end of a word is nearly always silent and it makes the preceding vowel long (the Final E Rule), as in "rode, side, cake." In a few words it doesn't affect the vowel, as in "come, some, carve, give, love."

le, en   The letter E is also silent in the digraphs LE and EN at the end of words like "principle" and "listen."

Silent Letter H

H = /silent/   hour, honor, honest, Thomas, rhyme

☞ **Note:** Words beginning with WH may or may not sound the /h/. For example, "where" can be pronounced with or without the H as /hwer/ or /wer/, but "who" is always just /ho͞o/.

Silent Letter L

LD = /d/   would, could, should

LF = /l/   half, calf

162

Silent Letter M

MN = /m/   autumn, column, hymn, damn, solemn

Silent Letter P

P = /silent/   corps, cupboard, receipt, raspberry, psychology, psalm

Silent Digraph PH

PH = /f/   phone, photograph, phonograph, pharmacy, phantom, Philadelphia, philosophy, phrase, physical, orphan, gopher, dolphin, hyphen

Note that P and H don't make their usual sounds.

Silent Letter Q(U)

Q = silent   queen, quarter, quart, quality, quick, question, quit, quiz

The letter Q is usually silent and occurs in the digraph QU to make the /k/ sound, as in "quick."

Silent Letter S

S = silent   island, aisle, debris, Illinois

Silent Letter T

TCH = /ch/   match, catch, switch, watch, kitchen
TEN = /n/   listen, often, fasten, soften
TLE = /l/   castle, whistle, wrestle

Silent Letter U

U = silent   guest, guess, guitar, guard, build, building, guilty, rogue, rouge, tongue (Also silent in QU digraph words such as "quick, quiet.")

163

Vowel Digraphs could be said to have a silent letter, as below.

ai = /$\bar{a}$/ as in "aid"

aw = /$\ddot{a}$/ as in "saw"

ay = /$\bar{a}$/ as in "say"

ea = /$\bar{e}$/ as in "eat"

ee = /$\bar{e}$/ as in "see"

ew = /$\overline{oo}$/ as in "new"

oa = /$\bar{o}$/ as in "oat"

oo = /$\overline{oo}$/ as in "moon"

oo = /$\breve{oo}$/ as in "look"

ow = /$\bar{o}$/ as in "own"

Odd Silent Letters

TH is silent in "asthma" and "clothes."

D is silent in "Wednesday."

☞ **Note:** There are a lot of silent letters in more difficult, seldom used, or technical words. Words imported into English from other languages often have silent letters. We see this in many last names (for example, Rousseau).

164

142 Silent Letters: WR

Note that these words all start with a silent W:

write, wrote, wrong, wreck, wrinkle, wrench, wring, wrist

☞ **DIRECTIONS:** Replace the silent letter and write a sentence using the word.

1. ____rite

_____

2. ____reck

_____

3. ____rong

_____

4. ____rinkle

_____

5. ____ring

_____

6. ____rench

_____

7. ____rote

_____

8. ____rist

_____

143 Silent Letters: GN

Note that these words all start with a silent G:

gnat, gnome, gnarl, gnash, gnaw

☞ **DIRECTIONS:** Replace the silent letter and write a sentence using the word.

1. _____nat

_____

2. _____nome

_____

3. _____narl

_____

4. _____nash

_____

5. _____naw

_____

Note that these words all start with a silent K:

know, knee, knife, knot, knack, knock, knob, knew

☞ **DIRECTIONS:** Replace the silent letter and write a sentence using the word.

1. ____now

_____

2. ____nee

_____

3. ____nife

_____

4. ____not

_____

5. ____nack

_____

6. ____nock

_____

7. ____nob

_____

8. ____new

_____

145 Silent Letters: Silent Blend GH

The letters GH are often called the "silent blend," so they do not contribute to the sound of the word. But these words are badly misspelled if the "silent blend" is missing.

☞ **DIRECTIONS:** Add the silent blend GH to these words so that they will be spelled correctly, say the word, and write it in a sentence.

hi_____ _____

rou_____ _____

li_____t _____

wei_____ _____

tou_____ _____

nei_____bor _____

bou_____t _____

cau_____t _____

dou_____ _____

dau_____ter _____

slei_____ _____

strai_____t _____

ni_____t _____

hei_____t _____

cou_____ _____

enou_____ _____

althou_____ _____

fou_____t _____

146 Silent Letters: Silent B and D

Several other letters are silent in some fairly common English words.

☞ **DIRECTIONS:** Fill in the missing letter in each of these words, say the word twice, and then write it in a sentence.

Silent B

dou____t _____

dum____ _____

lim____ _____

clim____ _____

com____ _____

bom____ _____

thum____ _____

de____t _____

Silent D

e____ge _____

ba____ge _____

fu____ge _____

he____ge _____

Review: Fill in the missing letter and say the word.

dum____   he____ge

e____ge   ba____ge

bom____   clim____

147 Silent Letters: Silent H and P

Several other letters are silent in some fairly common English words.

☞ **DIRECTIONS:** Fill in the missing letter in each of these words, say the word twice, and then write it in a sentence.

Silent H

____our _____

____onest _____

r____yme _____

____onor _____

Silent P

recei____t _____

ras____berry _____

cu____board _____

____sychology _____

Review: Fill in the missing letter and say the word.

____our   r____yme

cu____board   ____onest

____sychology   recei____t

____onor   ras____berry

148 Silent Letters: Silent PH and QU

Several other letters are silent in some fairly common English words.

☞ **DIRECTIONS:** Fill in the missing letters in each of these words, say the word twice, and then write it in a sentence.

PH = /f/ Sound

_____one _____

_____oto _____

go_____er _____

_____iladel_____ia _____

hy_____en _____

QU = /kw/ Sound

_____een _____

_____iz _____

_____it _____

_____arter _____

_____ick _____

Review: Fill in the missing letters and say the word.

_____one   _____oto

_____iz   _____arter

_____ick   _____it

_____een   _____iladel_____ia

149 Silent Letters: Silent T and U

Several other letters are silent in some fairly common English words.

☞ **DIRECTIONS:** Fill in the missing letter in each of these words, say the word twice, and then write it in a sentence.

Silent T

ma____ch _____

ca____ch _____

lis____en _____

of____en _____

cas____le _____

whis____le _____

Silent U

g____est _____

g____itar _____

b____ilding _____

tong____e _____

g____ess _____

g____ard _____

Review: Fill in the missing letter and say the word.

of____en   lis____en

g____ess   cas____le

b____ilding   g____itar

DOUBLE LETTERS

There are only four consonants that are frequently doubled:

F as in off

L as in full

S as in less

Z as in jazz

The problem for the writer is that the single consonant sometimes makes the same sound, for example, boss and gas.

The letter F is often doubled at the end of a word.

☞ **DIRECTIONS:** Fill in the missing letters in each of these words, say the word twice, and then write it in a sentence.

Double FF

1. cli____ _____

2. o____ _____

3. sta____ _____

4. blu____ _____

5. flu____ _____

6. pu____ _____

7. cu____ _____

8. stu____ _____

9. whi____ _____

10. sti____ _____

11. scu____ _____

12. sni____ _____

Review: Fill in the missing letters and say the word twice.

stu____ cu____

o____ sti____

cli____ blu____

flu____ scu____

151 Double Letters: LL

The letter L is often doubled at the end of a word.

☞ **DIRECTIONS:** Fill in the missing letters in each of these words, say the word twice, and then write it in a sentence.

Double LL

1. ba____ _____

2. du____ _____

3. a____ _____

4. be____ _____

5. fa____ _____

6. bu____ _____

7. to____ _____

8. ce____ _____

9. mi____ _____

10. ca____ _____

Review: Fill in the missing letters and say the word twice.

fa____   to____

be____   ca____

ce____   a____

ba____   mi____

152 Double Letters: SS

The letter S is often doubled at the end of a word.

☞ **DIRECTIONS:** Fill in the missing letters in each of these words, say the word twice, and then write it in a sentence.

1. cla____ _____

2. fu____ _____

3. ki____ _____

4. le____ _____

5. to____ _____

6. ba____ _____

7. ble____ _____

8. cro____ _____

9. bo____ _____

10. che____ _____

11. dre____ _____

12. gla____ _____

Review: Fill in the missing letters and say the word twice.

to____　　　　bo____

che____　　　ba____

le____　　　　ki____

fu____　　　　ble____

153 Double Letters: ZZ

The letter Z is often doubled at the end of a word.

☞ **DIRECTIONS:** Fill in the missing letters in each of these words, say the word twice, and then write it in a sentence.

1. fi_____ _____

2. ja_____ _____

3. fu_____ _____

4. bu_____ _____

The letter Z is also doubled at the end of a syllable in some words.

☞ **DIRECTIONS:** Fill in the missing letters in each of these words, say the word twice, and then write it in a sentence.

1. da_____le _____

2. pi_____a _____

3. pu_____le _____

4. dri_____le _____

5. mu_____le _____

Review: Fill in the missing letters and say the word twice.

ja_____   pu_____le

mu_____le   fi_____

da_____le   dri_____le

fu_____   bu_____

SUFFIXES

This section will concentrate on just one major spelling problem when adding suffixes: "When do you double the final consonant before adding the suffix?"

For example, which is correct when adding a suffix to _run_?

runing or _running_

runs or _runns_

The answer is in a rather complex spelling rule in Lessons 154 through 157. In fact it is so complex that you might not bother teaching it to younger children, so use your own judgment based on what you know about your students. But if you don't teach the rule, then you are stuck with a lot of individual words to teach.

154 Suffixes: Doubling Final Consonant

Suffixes can be a bit confusing, but here is the <u>basic doubling rule</u>: You double the final consonant when the word ends in a single consonant preceded by a single vowel and the suffix begins with a vowel.

For example, if you want to add the suffix ING to the word "run," you double the final N to make the correct spelling RUNNING.

RUN + ING = RU<u>NN</u>ING (Double letter.)

But if you want to add an S to RUN, you do not double the N because S is not a vowel.

RUN + S = RUNS (No double letter.)

☞ **DIRECTIONS:** Add ING or S to each of these words. Be careful to double the final consonant, but only if you need to.

Base Word	Adding ING	Adding S
Example: *run*	*running*	*runs*
1. cut		
2. bat		
3. plan		
4. hug		
5. ship		
6. hop		
7. get		
8. wet		

155 Suffixes: Doubling Two-Vowel Words

Here is the basic doubling rule again: You double the final consonant when the words end in a single consonant preceded by a *single* vowel and the suffix begins with a vowel. But you should watch out for a two-vowel word.

For example, if you want to add ING to READ: READ + ING = READING (No doubling because there are two vowels in the word.)

And if you want to add an S to READ, you do not double the D because S is not a vowel.

READ + S = READS (No double letter.)

☞ **DIRECTIONS:** Add ING or S to each of these words. Be careful to double the final consonant, but only if you need to.

Base Word	Adding ING	Adding S
Example: *read*	*reading*	*reads*
1. plan	_____	_____
2. rain	_____	_____
3. sleep	_____	_____
4. get	_____	_____
5. look	_____	_____
6. bat	_____	_____
7. paint	_____	_____
8. ship	_____	_____

156 Suffixes: Doubling Two Consonants at End

Here is the basic doubling rule again: You double the final consonant when the words end in a single consonant preceded by a single vowel and the suffix begins with a vowel.

Watch out for two consonants at the end of a word.

For example, if you want to add ING to SING:

SING + ING = SINGING (No doubling because SING has two consonants at the end.)

And if you want to add an S to SING, you do not double anything.

SING + S = SINGS (No double letter.)

☞ **DIRECTIONS:** Add ING or S to each of these words. Be careful to double the final consonant, but only if you need to.

Base Word	Adding ING	Adding S
Example: *sing*	*singing*	*sings*
1. find	_____	_____
2. plan	_____	_____
3. kick	_____	_____
4. hop	_____	_____
5. smart	_____	_____
6. get	_____	_____
7. paint	_____	_____
8. deal	_____	_____

157 Suffixes: Words Ending in E

Here is the basic doubling rule again: You double the final consonant when the words end in a single consonant preceded by a single vowel and the suffix begins with a vowel. But you should also watch out for words ending with the letter E.

For example, if you want to add ING to WRITE:

WRITE + ING = WRITING (No doubling, but you drop the E.)

But if you want to add the suffix S to a word ending in E, just add the S (don't drop the E.)

WRITE + S = WRITES

☞ **DIRECTIONS:** Add ING or S to each of these words. Be careful about whether or not you should drop the final E.

Base Word	Adding ING	Adding S
Example: *write*	*writing*	*writes*
1. give	_____	_____
2. live	_____	_____
3. bat	_____	_____
4. love	_____	_____
5. hug	_____	_____
6. race	_____	_____
7. trade	_____	_____
8. eye	_____	_____

COMPOUND WORDS

A compound word is a word spelled by putting two words together without a space between them. The compound word has a single meaning that might be a little different from the two words.

The problem for the speller is, "Is it a compound word or two words?"

The answer is, "When two words are very frequently used together, they become a compound word."

However, many times even dictionaries disagree with each other on the 'one word or two' problem.

158 Compound Words

A compound word is a word spelled by putting two words together without a space between them. The compound word has a single meaning that might be a little different from the two words.

The problem for the speller is "Is it a compound word or two words?" For example, "Why is 'sidewalk' a compound word while 'side dish' is two words?"

The answer is "When two words are very frequently used together, they become a compound word." However, many times even dictionaries disagree with each other on the 'one word or two' problem.

Study these examples: (read across)

Compound Word	Two Words
roommate	room clerk
someone	some fun
grandmother	grand master
inside	in between
downtown	down below

☞ **DIRECTIONS:** Decide whether these two words are a compound or two words, then write the correct word or words.

1. pan + cake _____

2. ticket + office _____

3. down + stairs _____

4. red + paint _____

5. corn + bread _____

6. round + trip _____

7. some + thing _____

8. low + rent _____

9. ball + field _____

10. front + door _____

Most prefixes are simply short meaning units put at the beginning of a word, like "un" as in "unhappy" or "re" as in "rewrite."

However, if the prefix is AD, or its many variations, you must double the first letter of the root. For example: _account_. See Lesson 159 for a better explanation.

Like the prefix AD, the first letter of the root must be doubled for a few other prefixes, such as CO. For example: _correct_.

Most prefixes are simply short meaning units put at the beginning of a word, like "un" as in "unhappy" or "re" as in "rewrite."

Double Letters for Prefixes. Many times the prefix AD meaning "to" or "toward" changes its spelling to letter A plus the first letter of the root. This causes a double letter (geminate), which really introduces a silent letter. For example:

AC   accident, account, access, accurate

AD   address, add, addict

AF   affect, affirm, affluence, affix, afford, affront

AG   aggregate, aggrieved, aggressive

AL   alliance, allergy, alley, alligator, allow

AN   annual, annex, announce, annoy, annul

AP   applause, appeal, apparel, appear, appendix, appetite, apple

AR   arrest, arrive, arrange, arrears, arrow

AS   asset, associate, assemble, association, assign, assist

AT   attach, attack, attend, attempt, attorney, attractive, attic

☞ **DIRECTIONS:** Fill in the missing letter or letters for these words. Refer to the words above for help.

1. _____rest

2. a_____nual

3. a_____ey

4. a_____le

5. a_____ist

6. a_____dress

7. at__ic

8. a_____ount

9. a_____ear

10. a_____row

160 Prefixes: Letter Doubling O- and CO-

Here are some other words in which the prefix uses a double letter:

office, officer, offer, offend, offense

oppose, opposite, opportunity

correct, corral, correspond, corrupt

collect, college, collar, collide

common, community, communicate, committees, commute

command, comment, commit, commerce, comma

☞ **DIRECTIONS:** Fill in the missing letter or letters for these words. Refer to the words above for help.

1. o_____fice

2. co_____rect

3. co_____al

4. o_____ose

5. co_____ittee

6. col_____ar

7. co_____ege

8. op_____osite

9. co_____a

10. co_____ect

ENDING SOUNDS

Ending sounds cause a lot of spelling errors. For example, is the ending sound /k/ spelled K or CK, as in <u>back</u> or <u>cook</u>?

This ending problem occurs with a lot of other words, such as the ending /r/ sound in <u>doctor</u>, <u>collar</u>, or <u>faster</u>.

There are not many rules to help you, except that the ER ending is always used in comparative adjectives.

Examples: big, *bigger*, biggest

cold, *colder*, coldest

161 Ending Sounds: LE = EL

The final sound /əl/ (or schwa plus /l/) causes a lot of spelling trouble because it can be spelled: LE as in "little" or EL as in "travel."

Unfortunately, there seems to be little reason why or when you use EL or LE, so you will just have to memorize the words. This lesson is just to make you more aware of the final /əl/ sound.

LE Words

angle
cattle
little
nibble
rattle
settle
table
turtle

EL Words

angel
bushel
gravel
level
model
motel
pretzel
travel

☞ **DIRECTIONS:** Fill in the correct last two letters and say the word. Watch out! The final two words are pronounced differently to give a different meaning.

1. tab_____   **5.** litt_____   **9.** sett_____   **13.** ratt_____

2. turt_____   **6.** bush_____   **10.** catt_____   **14.** lev_____

3. mot_____   **7.** trav_____   **11.** mod_____   **15.** ang_____

4. nibb_____   **8.** pretz_____   **12.** grav_____   **16.** ang_____

162 Ending Sounds: ER = AR = OR

The final sound /ər/ (or schwa plus /r/) causes a lot of spelling trouble because it can be spelled: ER as in "bigger," AR as in "dollar," or OR as in "actor."

Unfortunately, there seems to be little reason why or when you use ER, AR, or OR, so you will just have to memorize the words. This lesson is just to make you more aware of the final /ər/ sound.

ER Words	AR Words	OR Words
bigger	burglar	author
blister	collar	doctor
dreamer	dollar	editor
faster	grammar	flavor
freezer	lunar	motor
jogger	solar	tractor

☞ **DIRECTIONS:** Fill in the missing letters and say the word.

1. bigg_____   **5.** fav_____   **9.** dream_____   **13.** edit_____

2. doct_____   **6.** fast_____   **10.** gramm_____   **14.** freez_____

3. doll_____   **7.** sol_____   **11.** lun_____   **15.** tract_____

4. coll_____   **8.** jogg_____   **12.** blist_____   **16.** auth_____

163 Ending Sounds: ER = AR = OR

The final sound /ər/ (or schwa plus /r/) causes a lot of spelling trouble because it can be spelled: ER as in "bigger," AR as in "dollar," or OR as in "actor."

Unfortunately, there seems to be little reason why or when you use ER, AR, or OR, so you will just have to memorize the words. This lesson is just to make you more aware of the final /ər/ sound.

actor	steeper
beggar	sweeter
cheaper	teacher
director	thinner
gentler	trailer
river	voter
slower	waiter
smaller	worker
smarter	younger

☞ **DIRECTIONS:** Fill in the missing letters and say the word.

1. teach_____   **5.** smart_____   **9.** cheap_____   **13.** thinn_____

2. gentl_____   **6.** steep_____   **10.** small_____   **14.** trail_____

3. slow_____   **7.** act_____   **11.** vot_____   **15.** begg_____

4. sweet_____   **8.** wait_____   **12.** work_____   **16.** riv_____

164 Ending Sounds: K and CK

How do you spell the /k/ sound at the end of a word? Here are some suggestions: The /k/ sound is spelled CK at the end of a short word (one syllable and short vowel word).

For example, *back, lock*

But at the end of a two-vowel letter word (vowel digraph), the /k/ sound is spelled with just the letter K.

For example, *seek, soak, took, beak*

/k/ Spelled CK (Single-Vowel Words)

back	duck	quick
buck	flock	rock
black	jack	sick
block	kick	sock
check	knock	stick
chick	lock	suck
clock	luck	tack
dock	neck	tick
deck	pick	

/k/ Spelled K (Double-Vowel Words)

break	peak	steak
book	peek	took
cook	seek	weak
creak	shook	week
cheek	shriek	
crook	sneak	
nook	soak	
oak	speak	

☞ **DIRECTIONS:** Fill in the missing letters. Watch the ending.

1. You get paid with a ch_____.

2. An old roof may l_____.

3. You like to eat a st_____.

4. Finding a dollar is good l_____.

5. The opposite of white is bl_____.

6. A group of birds is a fl_____.

7. If a glass falls, it may bre_____.

8. You may like to read a b_____.

198

165 Ending Sounds: KE and NK

Here are two other word ending sounds that use the letter K and contain the /k/ sound.

Ending Spelled KE		
bake	like	spike
broke	take	spoke
cake	pike	stake
Coke	poke	strike
fake	quake	stroke
flake	rake	take
joke	shake	wake
lake	smoke	woke
make	snake	yoke

Ending Spelled NK		
bank	hank	spank
blank	ink	stank
blink	junk	stink
brink	mink	sunk
chunk	monk	tank
clink	pink	thank
crank	rank	think
dank	shrink	trunk
drink	skunk	yank
frank	slink	

☞ **DIRECTIONS:** Fill in the missing letters.

1. On your birthday you might eat ca_____ _____.

2. A large body of water may be a la_____ _____.

3. When you are thirsty, you need a dri_____ _____.

4. Keep your money in a ba_____ _____.

5. Don't pick up a rattlesna_____ _____.

6. Where there is fire, there is smo_____ _____.

7. You can keep a lot of water in a ta_____ _____.

8. You might not like the smell of a sku_____ _____.

SPELLING PROBLEMS

Here are a few other common sources of spelling problems:

1. −ion vs. −ssion or −sion, as in *education*, *mission*, or *mansion*.

2. When does the letter C make the /s/ sound and when does it make the /k/ sound?

3. When is the Long E /ē/ sound spelled IE and when is it spelled EI? For example, *chief* or *ceiling*?

4. When do you use the −AIR and when do you use the −ARE ending? For example, *chair* or *bare*?

166 Spelling Problems: Letter C

The letter C has no sound of its own.

The letter C make the /s/ sound before letters E, I, and Y (some call it a soft C).

The letter C makes the /k/ sound before letters A, O, and U (some call it a hard C).

C = /s/		C = /k/	
cent	pencil	can	score
cell	ice	come	second
cycle	fancy	car	become
city	acid	cut	American
circus	face	cold	because

☞ **DIRECTIONS:** In these words, write an S or a K to tell whether the letter C make the /s/ sound or the /k/ sound.

1. cent _____

2. cut _____

3. face _____

4. fancy _____

5. car _____

6. city _____

7. acid _____

8. come _____

9. because _____

10. pencil _____

11. can _____

12. second _____

167 Spelling Problems: IE or EI?

Do you spell the Long E sound IE or EI?

The Long E /e/ sound is usually spelled IE, but it is spelled EI after the letter C. The old rule is "I before E except after C."

Usual Spelling IE		**Spelled EI after C**
believe	priest	ceiling
brief	shield	conceited
chief	shriek	deceit
field	thief	receipt
grief	yield	receive

☞ **DIRECTIONS:** Fill in EI or IE to complete the word, then write the completed whole word.

Examples: *ch ____f* <u>*chief*</u>

1. rec____ve _____

2. l____sure _____

3. f____ld _____

4. sh____ld _____

5. th____f _____

6. bel____ve _____

7. br____f _____

8. c____ling _____

9. rec____ve _____

10. gr____f _____

11. ch____f _____

12. pr____st _____

168 Spelling Problems: -TION vs. -SION

There are several ways to spell the /shun/ sound at the end of many words, so pay attention to it. By far the most common is "TION."

TION		SSION	SION
action	election	aggression	expansion
application	fiction	commission	explosion
auction	graduation	confession	extension
collection	location	mission	mansion
connection	lotion	passion	pension
donation	location	profession	tension
education	lotion	session	version

☞ **DIRECTIONS:** Fill in the TION, SSION, or SION, then write the complete whole word and say it.

Example: na___   *nation*

1. ac_____   _____

2. educa_____   _____

3. se_____   _____

4. profe_____   _____

5. loca_____   _____

6. collec_____   _____

7. man_____   _____

8. auc_____   _____

9. elec_____   _____

10. pa_____   _____

11. mi_____   _____

12. explo_____   _____

169 Spelling Problems: -AIR vs. -ARE

Another source of spelling problems is the ending of words that end with AIR or ARE, since the ending sound is exactly the same.

-AIR	-ARE	
air	bare	rare
chair	blare	scare
fair	dare	share
flair	fare	snare
glair	flare	spare
hair	glare	square
lair	hare	stare
pair	mare	ware
stair	pare	

☞ **DIRECTIONS:** Fill in the AIR or ARE, then write the complete whole word and say it.

Example: *p_____*   *pair*

1. sc_____ _____

2. st_____ _____

3. ch_____ _____

4. r_____ _____

5. gl_____ _____

6. h_____ _____

7. fl_____ _____

8. b_____ _____

9. sh_____ _____

10. squ_____ _____

11. l_____ _____

12. sc_____ _____

HOMOPHONE LOOK-UP DRILLS

Introduction

These last lessons are to give you practice quickly looking up the spelling and meaning of many homophones in the Homophone Master List in the Appendix. Use the Guide Words at the top of every Master List page. Guide Words are the first and last words on a page. Many dictionaries and other alphabetized reference books have Guide Words because they save you time. If the word you are looking up is not between the two Guide Words, it is not on that page.

For example, if you want to find the homophone for "away" it will be on the first page, because the Guide Words on that page go from "acts" to "bawl."

But you won't find "jam" because "jam" is not alphabetically between the Guide Words "acts" to "bawl."

In listing the homophone pairs in the Master List, the more common word is listed first.

The Master List has a very brief meaning, meaning clue, or synonym for every word in parentheses following the homophone word. If you need a fuller definition or more multiple meanings, use a dictionary.

☞ **Note:** Teachers, you can occasionally add interest to these Look-Up drills by having students compete to see who can correctly finish the lesson page first.

170 Homophone Look-Up Drill

☞ **DIRECTIONS:**

1. Look up the base word using the Master List in the Appendix.
2. Write down the homophone.
3. Write the short meaning of the homophone.
4. Use it in a sentence.

Example:

ball   homophone: <u>bawl</u>   meaning: <u>to cry</u>
(round object)
sentence: <u>Some babies bawl when hungry.</u>

Base Word

1. ad   homophone: _____ meaning: _____
(advertisement)
sentence: _____.

2. boy   homophone: _____ meaning: _____
(male child)
sentence: _____.

3. cash   homophone: _____ meaning: _____
(money)
sentence: _____.

4. principle   homophone: _____ meaning: _____
(rule)
sentence: _____.

5. lesson   homophone: _____ meaning: _____
(instruction)
sentence: _____.

6. load   homophone: _____ meaning: _____
(burden)
sentence: _____.

171 Homophone Look-Up Drill

☞ **DIRECTIONS:**

1. Look up the base word using the Master List in the Appendix.
2. Write down the homophone.
3. Write the short meaning of the homophone.
4. Use it in a sentence.

Example:

overseas   homophone: <u>oversees</u>   meaning: <u>supervises</u>
(abroad)
sentence: <u>The manager of the company oversees his employees.</u>

Base Word

1. mall   homophone: _____   meaning: _____
(courtyard; group of shops)
sentence: _____.

2. eve   homophone: _____   meaning: _____
(evening)
sentence: _____.

3. fawn   homophone: _____   meaning: _____
(baby deer)
sentence: _____.

4. jam   homophone: _____   meaning: _____
(fruit jelly)
sentence: _____.

5. in   homophone: _____   meaning: _____
(opposite of *out*)
sentence: _____.

6. wait   homophone: _____   meaning: _____
(linger)
sentence: _____.

172 Homophone Look-Up Drill

☞ **DIRECTIONS:**

1. Look up the base word using the Master List in the Appendix.
2. Write down the homophone.
3. Write the short meaning of the homophone.
4. Use it in a sentence.

Example:

cue   homophone: <u>queue</u>   meaning: <u>line up</u>
(prompt)
sentence: <u>The queue to buy tickets at the movie theater was</u>
<u>very long.</u>

Base Word

1. who's   homophone: _____ meaning: _____
(who is)
sentence: _____.

2. real   homophone: _____ meaning: _____
(genuine)
sentence: _____.

3. hoard   homophone: _____ meaning: _____
(hidden supply)
sentence: _____.

4. chews   homophone: _____ meaning: _____
(bites)
sentence: _____.

5. chilly   homophone: _____ meaning: _____
(cold)
sentence: _____.

6. kernel   homophone: _____ meaning: _____
(grain of wheat or corn)
sentence: _____.

173 Homophone Look-Up Drill

☞ DIRECTIONS:

1. Look up the base word using the Master List in the Appendix.
2. Write down the homophone.
3. Write the short meaning of the homophone.
4. Use it in a sentence.

Example:

mall   homophone: <u>maul</u>   meaning: <u>attack</u>
(courtyard; group of shops)
sentence: <u>Bears will only maul humans if provoked.</u>

Base Word

1. sail   homophone: _____ meaning: _____
(travel by boat)
sentence: _____.

2. beach   homophone: _____ meaning: _____
(shore)
sentence: _____.

3. click   homophone: _____ meaning: _____
(small sound)
sentence: _____.

4. earn   homophone: _____ meaning: _____
(work for money)
sentence: _____.

5. have   homophone: _____ meaning: _____
(possess)
sentence: _____.

6. mat   homophone: _____ meaning: _____
(floor covering)
sentence: _____.

174 Homophone Look-Up Drill

☞ **DIRECTIONS:**

1. Look up the base word using the Master List in the Appendix.
2. Write down the homophone.
3. Write the short meaning of the homophone.
4. Use it in a sentence.

Example:

need   homophone: <u>knead</u>   meaning: <u>mix with hands</u>
(require)
sentence: <u>The baker kneaded the bread dough until it was smooth.</u>

Base Word

1. shake   homophone: _____ meaning: _____
(move from side to side)
sentence: _____.

2. shoot   homophone: _____ meaning: _____
(use a gun)
sentence: _____.

3. side   homophone: _____ meaning: _____
(flank)
sentence: _____.

4. steak   homophone: _____ meaning: _____
(meat)
sentence: _____.

5. lay   homophone: _____ meaning: _____
(recline)
sentence: _____.

6. aid   homophone: _____ meaning: _____
(assistance)
sentence: _____.

175 Homophone Look-Up Drill

☞ **DIRECTIONS:**

1. Look up the base word using the Master List in the Appendix.

2. Write down the homophone.

3. Write the short meaning of the homophone.

4. Use it in a sentence.

Example:

seller   homophone: <u>cellar</u>   meaning: <u>underground room</u>
(one who sells)
sentence: <u>Some people keep their old furniture stored in the</u>
<u>cellar.</u>

☞ **Note:** Some words have a second homophone.

Base Word

1. aisle   homophone: _____ meaning: _____
(path)

sentence: _____.

           homophone: _____ meaning: _____

sentence: _____.

2. doe   homophone: _____ meaning: _____
(female deer)

sentence: _____.

           homophone: _____ meaning: _____

sentence: _____.

176 Homophone Look-Up Drill

☞ **DIRECTIONS:**

1. Look up the base word using the Master List in the Appendix.
2. Write down the homophone.
3. Write the short meaning of the homophone.
4. Use it in a sentence.

Example:

fur   homophone: <u>fir</u>   meaning: <u>tree</u>
(animal covering)
sentence: <u>We had a picnic under the shade of a tall fir.</u>

Base Word

1. bell   homophone: _____ meaning: _____
(something you ring)
sentence: _____.

2. locks   homophone: _____ meaning: _____
(plural of lock)
sentence: _____.

3. lamb   homophone: _____ meaning: _____
(baby sheep)
sentence: _____.

4. shoot   homophone: _____ meaning: _____
(use a gun)
sentence: _____.

5. rumor   homophone: _____ meaning: _____
(gossip)
sentence: _____.

6. seen   homophone: _____ meaning: _____
(viewed)
sentence: _____.

177 Homophone Look-Up Drill

☞ **DIRECTIONS:**

1. Look up the base word using the Master List in the Appendix.
2. Write down the homophone.
3. Write the short meaning of the homophone.
4. Use it in a sentence.

Example:

great   homophone: <u>grate</u>   meaning: <u>grind</u>
(large)
sentence: <u>I grated carrots for the coleslaw.</u>

Base Word

1. pray   homophone: _____   meaning: _____
(worship)
sentence: _____.

2. profit   homophone: _____   meaning: _____
(benefit)
sentence: _____.

3. massed   homophone: _____   meaning: _____
(grouped)
sentence: _____.

4. minor   homophone: _____   meaning: _____
(juvenile)
sentence: _____.

5. Lou   homophone: _____   meaning: _____
(name)
sentence: _____.

6. hay   homophone: _____   meaning: _____
(dried grass)
sentence: _____.

216

178 Homophone Look-Up Drill

☞ DIRECTIONS:

1. Look up the base word using the Master List in the Appendix.

2. Write down the homophone.

3. Write the short meaning of the homophone.

4. Use it in a sentence.

Example:

ring   homophone: <u>wring</u>   meaning: <u>squeeze</u>
(circular band)
sentence: <u>I had to wring out the mop after cleaning the floor.</u>

Base Word

1. grown   homophone: _____ meaning: _____
(cultivated)
sentence: _____.

2. foul   homophone: _____ meaning: _____
(bad)
sentence: _____.

3. allowed   homophone: _____ meaning: _____
(permitted)
sentence: _____.

4. bolder   homophone: _____ meaning: _____
(more bold)
sentence: _____.

5. bored   homophone: _____ meaning: _____
(past tense of *bore*)
sentence: _____.

6. ceiling   homophone: _____ meaning: _____
(top of a room)
sentence: _____.

179 Homophone Look-Up Drill

☞ **DIRECTIONS:**

1. Look up the base word using the Master List in the Appendix.

2. Write down the homophone.

3. Write the short meaning of the homophone.

4. Use it in a sentence.

Example:

rap   homophone: <u>wrap</u>   meaning: <u>cover</u>
(hit; talk)
sentence: <u>You can wrap yourself in my scarf if you get cold.</u>

☞ **Note:** Some words have a second homophone.

Base Word

1. for   homophone: _____ meaning: _____
(in favor of)
sentence: _____.

            homophone: _____ meaning: _____

sentence: _____.

2. anti   homophone: _____ meaning: _____
(against)
sentence: _____.

            homophone: _____ meaning: _____

sentence: _____.

180 Homophone Look-Up Drill

👉 **DIRECTIONS:**

1. Look up the base word using the Master List in the Appendix.

2. Write down the homophone.

3. Write the short meaning of the homophone.

4. Use it in a sentence.

Example:

weak   homophone: <u>week</u>   meaning: <u>seven days</u>
(not strong)
sentence: <u>The teacher gave the students a week to complete</u>
<u>their homework assignment.</u>

Base Word

1. disk   homophone: _____ meaning: _____
(flat circular object)
sentence: _____.

2. cursor   homophone: _____ meaning: _____
(moving pointer)
sentence: _____.

3. feet   homophone: _____ meaning: _____
(plural of *foot*)
sentence: _____.

4. its   homophone: _____ meaning: _____
(possessive pronoun)
sentence: _____.

5. manner   homophone: _____ meaning: _____
(style)
sentence: _____.

6. pain   homophone: _____ meaning: _____
(discomfort)
sentence: _____.

APPENDIX: HOMOPHONE MASTER LIST

A

acts (deeds)
ax (tool)

ad (advertisement)
add (addition)

ads (advertisements)
adz (axe-like tool)

aid (assistance)
aide (a helper)

ail (be sick)
ale (beverage)

air (oxygen)
heir (successor)

aisle (path)
I'll (I will)
isle (island)

all (everything)
awl (a tool)

all together (in a group)
altogether (completely)

allowed (permitted)
aloud (audible)

already (previous)
all ready (all are ready)

alter (change)
altar (in a church)

ant (insect)
aunt (relative)

anti (against)
ante (before)
auntie (informal of *aunt*)

ark (boat)
arc (part of a circle)

ascent (climb)
assent (agree)

assistance (help)
assistants (those who help)

attendance (presence)
attendants (escorts)

away (gone)
aweigh (clear anchor)

awful (terrible)
offal (entrails)

B

bail (throw water out)
bale (bundle)

bait (lure)
bate (to decrease)

bald (no hair)
bawled (cried)

ball (round object)
bawl (cry)

band (plays music)
banned (forbidden)

barred (having bars)
bard (poet)

basil (an herb)
basal (fundamental)

baring (uncovering)
bearing (manner, machine)

bark (dog's sound)
barque (ship)

barren (no fruit)
baron (nobleman)

base (lower part)
bass (deep tone)

based (at a base)
baste (cover with liquid)

bases (plural of *base*)
basis (foundation)

bask (warm feeling)
Basque (country)

be (exist)
bee (insect)

beach (shore)
beech (tree)

bear (animal)
bare (nude)

beat (whip)
beet (vegetable)

been (past participle of *be*)
bin (box)

beer (drink)
bier (coffin)

beetle (insect)
Beadle (parish officer)

bell (something you ring)
belle (pretty woman)

berry (fruit)
bury (put in ground)

better (more good)
bettor (one who bets)

birth (born)
berth (bunk)

bite (chew)
byte (computer unit)
bight (slack part of rope)

bizarre (odd)
bazaar (market)

block (cube; obstruct)
bloc (group)

blue (color)
blew (did blow)

bolder (more bold)
boulder (big stone)

border (boundary)
boarder (one who boards)

222

bore (drill; be tiresome)
boar (hog)

bored (past tense of *bore*)
board (piece of wood)

born (delivered at birth)
borne (carried)
bourn (ending point)

bouillon (clear broth)
bullion (uncoined gold or silver)

bow (decorative knot)
beau (boyfriend)

bow (of a ship)
bough (of a tree)

bowl (dish; game)
boll (cotton pod)

boy (male child)
buoy (floating marker)

bread (food)
bred (cultivated)

break (smash)
brake (stop)

brewed (steeped)
brood (flock)

bridal (relating to a bride)
bridle (headgear for a horse)

Britain (country)
Briton (Englishperson)

brooch (pin)
broach (bring up)

brows (hairlines above eyes)
browse (to look through)

bruise (an injury)
brews (steeps)

build (construct)
billed (did bill)

bunt (bat gently in baseball)
bundt (ring-shaped cake)

burrow (dig)
burro (donkey)
borough (town)

but (except)
butt (end)

buy (purchase)
by (near)
bye (farewell)

C

cache (hiding place)
cash (money)

callus (hard tissue)
callous (unfeeling)

cannon (big gun)
canon (law)

can't (not able to)
cant (insincere statement)

canvas (cloth)
canvass (survey)

capital (money; city)
Capitol (U.S. Congress building)

carrot (vegetable)
carat (weight of precious stone)
caret (proofreader's mark)

carol (song)
carrel (study space at library)

cast (throw; list of actors)
caste (social class)

cause (origin)
caws (crow calls)

ceiling (top of a room)
sealing (closing)

censor (ban)
sensor (detection device)
censer (incense container)

cent (penny)
scent (odor)
sent (did send)

cents (pennies)
sense (clear thinking)

cereal (relating to grain)
serial (of a series)

chance (luck)
chants (songs)

chased (did chase)
chaste (modest)

cheap (inexpensive)
cheep (bird call)

chews (bites)
choose (select)

chic (style)
sheik (Arab chief)

chilly (cold)
chili (hot pepper)

choir (singers)
quire (amount of paper)

claws (nails on animal's feet)
clause (part of a sentence)

click (small sound)
clique (small exclusive group)

climb (ascend)
clime (climate)

close (shut)
clothes (clothing)
cloze (test)

clue (evidence; hint)
clew (ball of thread, yarn)

coal (fuel)
cole (cabbage)

coarse (rough)
course (school subject; path)

compliment (praise)
complement (complete set)

coop (chicken pen)
coupe (car)

coral (reef)
choral (music)

cord (string)
chord (musical notes)

core (center)
corps (army group)

corral (pen for livestock)
chorale (chorus)

correspondence (letters)
correspondents (writers)

council (legislative body)
counsel (advise)

cousin (relative)
cozen (deceive)

creak (grating noise)
creek (stream)

cruel (hurting)
crewel (stitching)

cruise (sail)
crews (groups of workers)
cruse (small pot)

cue (prompt)
queue (line up)

current (recent; part of stream)
currant (small raisin)

cursor (moving pointer)
curser (one who curses)

D

dam (wall to hold back water)
damn (to condemn or curse)

days (plural of day)
daze (in a foggy condition)

dear (greeting; loved one)
deer (animal)

dessert (follows main meal)
desert (abandon)

die (expire)
dye (color)

dine (eat)
dyne (unit of force)

discreet (unobtrusive)
discrete (noncontinuous)

disk (flat circular object)
disc (flat circular object)

disperse (scatter)
disburse (pay out)

doe (female deer)
dough (baking mixture)
do (musical note)

do (to perform or carry out)
due (something owed)
dew (drops of moisture)

225

done (finished)
dun (demand for payment)

ducked (did duck)
duct (tube)

duel (formal combat)
dual (two)

E

earn (work for money)
urn (container)

eight (number 8)
ate (did eat)

epic (great size; long poem)
epoch (period of time)

eve (evening)
eave (overhang on roof edge)

eye (organ of sight)
I (pronoun)
aye (yes)

F

faint (weak)
feint (pretend attack)

fair (honest; bazaar)
fare (cost of transportation)

fawn (baby deer)
faun (mythical creature)

faze (upset)
phase (stage)

feet (plural of *foot*)
feat (accomplishment)

feign (pretend)
fain (gladly)

find (discover)
fined (penalty of money)

flare (flaming signal)
flair (talent)

flea (insect)
flee (run away)

flew (did fly)
flu (influenza)
flue (shaft)

flow (moving along smoothly)
floe (sheets of floating ice)

flower (bloom)
flour (milled grain)

for (in favor of)
four (number 4)
fore (front part)

forward (front part)
foreword (preface)

fort (protective building)
forte (part of a sword)

fourth (after third)
forth (forward)

foul (bad)
fowl (bird)

frank (honest)
franc (French money)

freeze (cold)
frees (to free)
frieze (sculptured border)

fryer (frying chicken)
friar (brother in religious order)

fur (animal covering)
fir (tree)

G

gamble (to risk money)
gambol (to skip about)

gate (fence opening)
gait (foot movement)

gorilla (animal)
guerrilla (irregular soldier)

great (large)
grate (grind)

grown (cultivated)
groan (moan)

guessed (surmised)
guest (company)

guilt (opposite of innocence)
gilt (golden)

H

hail (ice; salute)
hale (healthy)

hair (strand-like growth on skin)
hare (rabbit)

hall (passage)
haul (carry)

handsome (attractive)
hansom (carriage)

hanger (to hang things on)
hangar (storage building)

have (possess)
halve (cut in half)

hay (dried grass)
hey (said to get attention)

hear (listen)
here (this place)

heard (listened)
herd (group of animals)

heart (body organ)
hart (male deer)

he'd (he would)
heed (pay attention)

heel (back part of foot)
he'll (he will)
heal (make well)

hi (hello)
high (opposite of *low*)
hie (to move quickly)

higher (above)
hire (employ)

227

him (pronoun)
hymn (religious song)

hoard (hidden supply)
horde (crowd)

hole (opening)
whole (complete)

holy (sacred)
holey (full of holes)
wholly (all)

horse (animal)
hoarse (husky voice)

hostile (unfriendly)
hostel (lodging for youth)

hour (sixty minutes)
our (possessive pronoun)

hurdle (jump over)
hurtle (throw)

hurts (pain)
hertz (unit of wave frequency)

hue (color)
hew (carve)

I

idle (lazy)
idol (god)
idyll (charming scene)

in (opposite of *out*)
inn (small hotel)

insight (self knowledge)
incite (cause)

instance (example)
instants (short periods of time)

insure (protect against loss)
ensure (make sure)

intense (extreme)
intents (aims)

islet (very small island)
eyelet (small hole for thread)

its (possessive pronoun)
it's (it is)

J

jam (fruit jelly)
jamb (window part)

jean (cotton cloth for pants)
gene (part of chromosome)

K

kernel (grain of wheat or corn)
colonel (military rank)

knit (weave with yarn)
nit (louse egg)

L

lamb (baby sheep)
lam (hiding)

lane (narrow way)
lain (past participle of *lie*)

lay (recline)
lei (necklace of flowers)

lead (metal)
led (guided)

leak (escaping through a crack)
leek (vegetable)

lean (incline; slender)
lien (claim)

least (smallest)
leased (rented)

lesson (instruction)
lessen (make less)

levee (embankment)
levy (funds collected by force)

liar (untruthful)
lyre (musical instrument)

lie (falsehood)
lye (alkaline solution)

liken (compare)
lichen (fungus)

lightning (occurs with thunder)
lightening (become light)

load (burden)
lode (vein or ore)

loan (something borrowed)
lone (single)

locks (plural of *lock*)
lox (smoked salmon)

loot (steal)
lute (musical instrument)

Lou (name)
lieu (instead of)

low (not high; cattle sound)
lo (interjection)

M

made (manufactured)
maid (servant)

mail (send by post)
male (masculine)

main (most important)
Maine (state)
mane (hair)

mall (courtyard; group of shops)
maul (attack)

manner (style)
manor (estate)

mantel (over fireplace)
mantle (cloak)

marry (join together)
merry (happy, joyful)
Mary (name)

marshal (law officer)
martial (militant)

massed (grouped)
mast (support)

mat (fibrous floor covering)
matte (dull surface)

maybe (perhaps, adj.)
may be (is possible, v.)

maze (network of passages)
maize (Indian corn)

meat (beef)
meet (make contact with)
mete (distribute equally)

medal (award)
meddle (interfere)

might (may; strength)
mite (small insect)

minor (juvenile)
miner (coal digger)

missed (failed to attain)
mist (fog)

moan (groan)
mown (cut down)

morn (morning, early day)
mourn (grieve)

morning (early day)
mourning (process of grieving)

mowed (cut down)
mode (fashion)

muscle (fibrous body tissue)
mussel (shellfish)

N

navel (depression on abdomen)
naval (nautical)

need (require)
knead (mix with hands)

neigh (whinny of horse)
nay (no)

new (not old)
knew (past tense of *know*)
gnu (animal)

night (evening)
knight (feudal warrior)

no (negative)
know (familiar with)

none (not any)
nun (religious sister)

not (in no manner)
knot (tangle)

O

one (number 1)
won (triumphed)

or (conjunction)
oar (paddle for a boat)
ore (mineral deposit)

oral (by mouth)
aural (by ear)

overdo (go to extremes)
overdue (past due)

overseas (abroad)
oversees (supervises)

owe (be indebted)
oh (exclamation)

owed (did owe)
ode (poem)

P

pail (bucket)
pale (without much color)

pain (discomfort)
pane (window glass)

pair (two of a kind)
pear (fruit)
pare (peel)

palate (roof of mouth)
palette (board for paint)
pallet (tool)

passed (went by)
past (former)

patience (composure)
patients (sick persons)

pause (brief stop)
paws (feet of animals)

peace (tranquility)
piece (part)

peak (mountaintop)
peek (quick look)
pique (to be upset)

peal (burst of noise, to ring)
peel (remove skin or rind)

pearl (jewel)
purl (knitting stitch)

pedal (ride a bike)
peddle (sell)

pie (kind of dessert)
pi (Greek letter)

pier (dock)
peer (equal)

plain (simple)
plane (airplane; flat surface)

plate (dish)
plait (braid)

please (to be agreeable)
pleas (plural of *plea*)

plum (fruit)
plumb (lead weight)

pole (stick)
poll (opinions; voting place)

pour (flow freely)
pore (skin gland, n; ponder, v.)

pray (worship)
prey (victim)

presents (gifts)
presence (appearance)

principal (chief)
principle (rule)

profit–wry

profit (benefit)
prophet (seer)

purr (cat sound)
per (for each)

R

rack (framework, shelf)
wrack (ruin)

rain (precipitation)
reign (royal authority)
rein (harness)

raise (put up)
rays (of sun)
raze (tear down)

rap (hit; talk)
wrap (cover)

read (peruse)
reed (plant)

read (perused)
red (color)

real (genuine)
reel (spool)

reek (give off strong odor)
wreak (inflict)

rest (relax)
wrest (force)

review (look back)
revue (musical)

rhyme (same end sound)
rime (ice covering; rhyme)

right (correct)
write (inscribe)
rite (ceremony)

ring (circular band)
wring (squeeze)

road (street)
rode (transported)
rowed (used oars)

roll (turn over; bread)
role (actor's character)

root (part of a plant)
route (highway)

rose (flower)
rows (lines)

rough (uneven, crude)
ruff (16th-/17th-century collar)

row (line, n.; use oars, v.)
roe (fish eggs)

rude (impolite)
rued (was sorry)

rumor (gossip)
roomer (renter)

rung (past tense of *ring;* ladder step)
wrung (squeezed)

rye (grain)
wry (ironic humor; twisted)

232

S

sack (bag)
sac (baglike object)

sail (travel by boat)
sale (bargain)

sea (ocean)
see (visualize)

sear (singe)
seer (prophet)

seed (part of a plant)
cede (grant)

seem (appear to be)
seam (joining mark)

seen (viewed)
scene (setting)

sell (receive money for merchandise)
cell (small room in prison; tiny part of living organism)

seller (one who sells)
cellar (underground room)

session (meeting)
cession (yield)

sew (mend)
so (in order that)
sow (plant)

shake (move from side to side)
sheik (Arab chief)

sheer (transparent)
shear (cut)

shoe (foot covering)
shoo (drive away)

shoot (use a gun)
chute (trough; slide)

shown (exhibited)
shone (beamed)

side (flank)
sighed (audible breath)

sight (see)
site (location)
cite (summon to court)

sign (signal)
sine (trigonometric function)

skull (head bones)
scull (boat; row)

slay (kill)
sleigh (sled)

slew (killed)
slue (swamp)

slight (slender)
sleight (dexterity)

some (portion)
sum (total)

son (male offspring)
sun (star)

sore-through

sore (painful)
soar (fly)

soul (spirit; essential part)
sole (one; bottom of foot/shoe)

stair (step)
stare (look intently)

stationery (paper)
stationary (fixed)

stayed (remained)
staid (proper)

steak (meat)
stake (post)

steal (rob)
steel (metal)

step (walk)
steppe (grassland prairie without trees, usually of Europe or Asia)

straight (not crooked)
strait (channel of water)

style (fashion)
stile (gate)

surf (waves)
serf (feudal servant)

surge (sudden increase)
serge (fabric)

sweet (sugary)
suite (connected rooms)

symbol (sign)
cymbal (percussion instrument)

T

tail (animal's appendage)
tale (story)

taper (to diminish)
tapir (animal)

taught (did teach)
taut (tight)

tax (assess; burden)
tacks (plural of *tack*)

tea (drink)
tee (holder for golf ball)

team (crew)
teem (be full)

tear (cry)
tier (level)

tear (rip apart)
tare (weight deduction)

tease (mock)
teas (plural of *tea*)

there (at that place)
their (possessive pronoun)
they're (they are)

there's (there is)
theirs (possessive pronoun)

threw (tossed)
through (finished)

234

thrown (tossed)
throne (royal's seat)

tick (insect; sound of clock)
tic (twitch)

tied (bound)
tide (ebb and flow of ocean)

time (duration)
thyme (herb)

to (toward)
too (also)
two (number 2)

toe (digit on foot)
tow (pull)

told (informed)
tolled (rang)

tool (helps you do a job)
tulle (silk net for veils)

towed (pulled)
toad (frog, usually in a dry habitat)

tray (used to carry things)
trey (domino or die with three dots)

troop (company, group of people)
troupe (group of performers)

trust (confidence)
trussed (tied)

turn (rotate)
tern (sea bird)

V

veil (face covering)
vale (valley)

vein (blood vessel)
vain (conceited)
vane (wind indicator)

very (absolutely)
vary (change)

vice (bad habit)
vise (clamp)

vile (disgusting)
vial (small bottle)

W

waist (middle of the body)
waste (trash)

wait (linger)
weight (heaviness)

want (desire)
wont (custom)

wave (moving swell of water)
waive (forgive or forego)

way (road)
weigh (measure heaviness)
whey (watery part of milk)

we (pronoun)
wee (small)

weak (not strong)
week (seven days)

wear–you're

wear (have on)
where (what place)
ware (items for sale)

weather (state of atmosphere)
whether (if)

weave (interlace)
we've (we have)

we'd (we would)
weed (plant)

weighed (measured heaviness)
wade (walk in water)

weighs (heaviness)
ways (plural of way)

we'll (we will)
wheel (circular frame)
weal (prosperity)

we're (we are)
weir (dam)

wet (moist)
whet (sharpen)

whale (sea mammal)
wail (cry)

which (what one)
witch (sorceress)

while (during)
wile (deceiving in a cunning way)

whine (complaining sound)
wine (drink made from grapes)

who's (who is)
whose (possessive of *who*)

wood (beneath bark of tree)
would (is willing to)

worst (most bad)
wurst (sausage)

Y

yolk (center of an egg)
yoke (harness)

you (pronoun)
ewe (female sheep)
yew (evergreen tree)

you'll (you will)
yule (Christmas)

your (possessive pronoun)
you're (you are)

CPSIA information can be obtained at www.ICGtesting.com
Printed in the USA
BVOW09s1629110814

362205BV00018B/44/P